A CONVICTED STOCK MANIPULATORS GUIDE TO INVESTING

A Convicted Stock Manipulators Guide to Investing

Marino Specogna

Writer's Showcase

New York Lincoln Shanghai

A Convicted Stock Manipulators Guide to Investing

Writer's Showcase
an imprint of iUniverse, Inc.

For information address:
iUniverse, Inc.
2021 Pine Lake Road, Suite 100
Lincoln, NE 68512
www.iuniverse.com

ISBN: 0-595-26466-2

Printed in the United States of America

I dedicate this to my wonderful, understanding, strong wife Natalie, my two awesome daughters, and my incredible family.

"We can't solve problems by using the same kind of thinking we used when we created them."

—Albert Einstein

Contents

Preface

A brief introduction on myself, to establish my credentials is provided initially. Then I provide a thorough description of typical deals to avoid with detailed information on how to spot certain shenanigans that should make you wary of a particular stock and thus avoid investing in it. I will tell you there is no other book with this information and after reading it you will know more about manipulated deals than any stock analyst, the general public and any enforcement agency.

Where to start?

Some information on myself would be a good starting point. This will help establish my credibility in regards to the information I am putting forward.

My name is Marino Specogna. I was born on the remote Queen Charlotte Islands of British Columbia, Canada. This previous sentence has been repeated in this manner a few times in the past before tribunals and judges. I think it is a good introduction. I was found guilty of a number of Securities Law violations locally in British Columbia, Canada. I was found guilty of stock market manipulation, of failing to file Insider Trading reports, of distributing securities without a prospectus exemption, and guilty of a number of other allegations including that I had traded well over 60% of a particular company's outstanding stock.

The local Securities Commission, found me guilty after a prolonged investigation from 1989 to 1994, and a resulting proceeding before a Securities Commission Tribunal. The Tribunal consisted of three members of the Securities Commission. The Securities Commission took a period of seven years from the initial investigation commencing to the sentence being delivered after the Tribunal. The Tribunal hearing took place over a five day period in 1994. The decision was reserved by the hearing chairperson, to a later date, that later date occurred in 1996.

During the time from 1994 until 1996, I had agreed to a temporary Cease Trade ban in a particular company. I had agreed in 1994 just before the Tribunal hearing commenced to this temporary ban. I agreed to a temporary ban for two reasons, one was to delay the hearing to a few months later, buy me time, and the other was to throw the Commission into believing myself to be a gullible market participant. The two year time from the end of the hearing up to the decision being returned, was a time period of my exploiting the system put into effect by the local Securities Commission. In the Decision returned by the Hearing Panel the term egregious was used to describe me, not a very complimentary term.

Most shocking would have to be the decision, a 20 year trading ban and a 20 year prohibition from acting as a director or officer of a reporting issuer in the Province of British Columbia Canada, and penalties in the form of a fine and costs.

The ban was shocking due to the fact all the high profile Securities Commission decisions before my Hearing and after my Hearing always returned more lenient bans and on the odd occasion stiffer financial fines. One prominent individual accused of defrauding over 10,000 investors, of over 200 million Canadian dollars was only given a 10 year stock trading ban in British Columbia. Let me identify the individual as F. B. since his case is progressing before the court system. F. B. it should be noted, that the firm he controlled spent money on personal items right out of the company bank account. At one point for six months, the company had a short television ad before the most watched newscast in British Columbia. I myself could not believe the ads with the references made in regards to the promised high interest rate of returns and wondered why the firm was not disciplined sooner for placing the ads. With my knowledge, I knew the firm to be a scam deal. The company was put into receivership by the local authorities finally after the Accounting firm that conducted the Audits relayed the audit information.

The term egregious is the term not used by the Commission to describe any other convicted manipulator, promoter, or stockbroker. In any other decision returned by the Securities Commission, egregious has never been used since, or before. It suggests I was the biggest stock manipulator to be tried by the B.C. Securities Commission. I am viewed as the most notorious stock manipulator in the history of the British Columbia securities market and have been vilified by the Commission and the industry. The Securities Commission investigators and lawyers were so incensed with my actions and behavior before the three panel members that they could not think straight. In fact, my actions and behavior before and after the Hearing disturbed the lawyers and investigators just as much.

The fun did not end there; two other proceedings resulted from this investigation and process. I was charged by the Securities Commission investigator with breach of three Securities Act violations in Provincial Court. Usually these types of charges are filed by a police force, in British Columbia, it would have been the Royal Canadian Mounted Police, ("RCMP").

These three charges formed a part of the Securities hearing and were heard a year before the charges were laid. Two years after the Securities hearing, a decision was returned. In the decision, I was found to have committed the three charges with all the additional charges made by the Securities Commission. However, in the Provincial Court hearing a plea agreement was struck where I would plead guilty to the one count of failing to file insider trading reports.

This plea agreement was reached because the Crown attorney did not believe sufficient evidence existed for the other two charges that were laid. The Crown representing the Provincial Government did not believe evidence existed for the charges. Out of all the allegations made by the Securities Commission, they put forth the three charges they believed they had enough evidence to prosecute with, but the Crown could not prosecute on the evidence the Securities Commission garnered. Not because of some Law that forbids disclosure but simply because a lower standard of proof exists in a Securities Commission procedure. In a real court, standards have to be maintained.

The Crown reviewed the Securities Commission information and no one, not even investigators with the Securities Commission or the RCMP Commercial Crimes Section could understand what had taken place in regards to relating the charges and the activities taking place. They knew I had accounted for the majority of the stock trading in the particular deal, trading millions of shares, but did not understand what it meant.

The only reason no one could understand what had taken place was the fact that none of these people had ever been involved in the Securities Market. None of them had ever tried to deceive or beat the system that exists. They were all working on theories and information that, past supposed manipulators, had previously provided some clues to manipulations when these earlier manipulators had previously pled guilty to manipulation schemes.

I will reiterate the following fact. You are learning from the most notorious and best stock manipulator. This fact is the main distinguishing difference that you as a reader will have over others who have not read this book. Of course, the exception being the manipulators out in the world who continue to manipulate markets and have not been caught. After you finish this book you will be able to interpret daily stock trading action where the tricks and manipulations disclosed in this book are visible and learn to avoid them to save your investing dollars.

If there has ever been an expert in market manipulation, and securities frauds it has to be me. In this small book, I give you all there is to know, all the insight into the securities markets and the factors of fraud and scam deals that you can apply to the real world. I will expose the different types of scams and manipulations, which really are the same in British Columbia, Canada as they are in New York, USA or London, UK or Moscow, Russia. The same basic factors and principles I outline are involved in a market manipulation, stock scam, everywhere in the world.

Introduction

Please note that not all manipulations are based on small cap or junior non-earnings corporations. Manipulations occur everyday in many stocks even supposed blue chip stock deals.

How is it that only after a scam stock or scheme stock has run the full course from moving to a high price to slumping back to a low price with all the dirty laundry being exposed after the fact, that suddenly every expert in the world appears and slams the particular stock in the media? Always after the fact when everyone knows the deal is a scam, a sham, and a scheme, do these supposed experts come forward and announce the obvious. If the so called experts were such experts why couldn't they voice the news well before individual investors, your mother, your father, your son, your daughter, your grandmother, your grandfather or yourself had fallen victim to a stock manipulation?

The reason is that a real expert would have conducted a stock manipulation before and knew the workings of a stock manipulation. A lot of the information I am providing in this book is not known to analysts or the general public or enforcement officials. The sole reason being that if you have not been in a situation to conduct a manipulation, to avoid detection, how is a person going to understand how a manipulation occurs or what particular signs or facts or trading tricks to look for. If you have never been involved in a manipulation then how can you possibly even fathom how to do a manipulation, or what the factors of a manipulation are or how the manipulation works or what forms a real manipulation, or what is a true manipulation?

From all the information and insights provided in this book, you can apply the information in your own research to find if any company financial statement information is being hidden, falsified, or misleading, or if any of the stock manipulation tricks are being utilized in the daily trading of a particular stock. Any of the outlined factors would suggest an attempted manipulation or a manipulation in progress. All the factors present would definitely suggest you avoid a stock you are researching, or own or, not advised by the author, possibly even play the deal knowing the deal is being manipulated. This last point has many pitfalls described later.

Some Basic Author facts

So I am not vilified or viewed too much as a scoundrel by you the reader, I want you to know about my background which you can view in the About the Author section. To summarize, my father had been involved in mineral exploration and had discovered the largest known Gold deposit in Western Canada, helping me gain interest in mineral exploration then stock promotion and financing.

My father became so successful that he floated a public company exploring for minerals in the early 1980's. That was a successful program from a geological basis as another new discovery was made that returned a nice high-grade small gold deposit on Vancouver Island, British Columbia.

From a stock market perspective the company was a bit of a dude, small float of less than 2 million shares issued, financing from $0.25 per share and running to over $2.00 per share, then falling to hardly trade due to no market making, no promotion of the company or it's projects. The main reason deals run so high is explained later on in this book. It relates to the theory of Supply and Demand, truly a proven theory.

Back in the early 1980's my father never thought of the theory he just believed if he did his best, applied himself and used his hard gained knowledge that when he struck it rich with a discovery he would strike it rich. Well to do that, you have to remember to sell some stock and cash out; this latter point is the basis of this book. Usually to sell there has to be a demand created for a stock, requiring promotion and a lot of times manipulative trading tricks.

I decided to help my father, I noticed with his ideas and thinking and way of working he was successful in one area but attention had to be paid to managing a junior company. I took a college diploma in Mining Engineering Technology all the while learning the ins and outs of managing a junior public company. Each year sometime 2 or 3 times in a year, new regulations were being heaped on public companies locally, most of the regulations just made it more expensive to work, requiring a company to pay more for accountants and lawyers, filing fees, trust company fees.

In some cases these days the majority of funds raised by a public small capitalized ("small cap") company go to paying administrative costs, hardly helping an individual investor relying on management scoring a nice big discovery or producing a new product. High management fees and expenses shown in Financial Statements usually translate to no work being done in remote areas to find minerals. The whole premise of a junior exploration or mining company is to raise funds to finance the exploration of prospects of minerals to delineate a mineable deposit. This premise of financing a company to use the funds to realize some earnings from producing a product or service is what a true public company is about. To be a truly public company the shares also have to be owned by the public.

Great fortunes can be made on a new discovery, but those happen very few between. The 1980's and 1990's saw quite a few new discoveries some very large discoveries, it could be classified as a prosperous time period for these particular types of companies. From 1992 to 1995, two major huge discoveries were made in two remote areas of Canada. In 1992, the first diamonds were found in Canada in the present day Nunavut Territory. The mine makes over $400 million annually. In 1995, Diamond Fields had discovered a huge nickel deposit in eastern Newfoundland; the deal was taken over by INCO for over $4.0 billion.

Eventually the amount of regulation seems to have led to junior mining companies raising funds just to pay accountants, lawyers, and regulatory fees. Mark my word now in 2002 that I doubt any major new mining discovery led by a Canadian junior mining company will occur, unless its in the diamond exploration field.

Eventually after graduation of college and wanting to learn how to promote a company I was let loose onto the local market scene. Vancouver was a smaller city then, just starting to grow into the metropolitan center it has become today. The local securities market, being the way it was, and the type of deals it financed produced a lot of characters, and during this time period in the mid 1980's there were many around.

The reason there were so many colorful characters around during this time period would have been because a few significant gold, diamond, and base metals discoveries had occurred and this attracted bizarre promoters from around the world. Many of the characters were undoubtedly molded over the years by the workings of the Exchange and the industry. The characteristics displayed in the characters currently being thrown into the limelight in the United States, due to all the recent Insider trading scandals, and the pillaging of blue chip company funds, are identifiable to me because these are similar characteristics of both the losers and crooks I was subjected to during the mid 1980's to mid 1990's.

If all the information I have disclosed in this book had been available a few years ago, maybe there would have been more scrutiny of the boom in the stock market financings, promotions, and highflying stock prices. Scams would have been found out sooner than later by enforcement agencies around the world and the amount of money lost to individuals would have been kept to a low amount.

Somehow, I know through human nature that would not have been the case. Even now, as you read this small informative book, someone else reading it will think nothing of the information, will believe it to be fantasy, to be a silly book. I assure you someone who will not even read the information contained in this book will pipe up and scream the author does not know diddlysquat about anything, and try to discredit this information. I assure you the facts are for real, the manipulations are real, and my notoriety is real.

I do know a lot, and I will tell you it all. If I was not such a notorious scoundrel of a stock manipulator, I certainly would not have been called egregious and I certainly would not have been found guilty of stock manipulation, and distributing shares without an exemption. You read and learn.

Vancouver, Canadian and American Stock Deals

When I first was let loose on Vancouver's Howe Street, Wow did my eyes open up. Of course being green and naïve and new to anything the first people you run into are always looking to take advantage of you. Most are down on their luck desperados or seasoned bandits and manipulators.

The biggest obstacle is to overcome your innocence and way of thinking. Sure, I was hoodwinked a few times out of a few grand here and there, but I would hangout with the big promoters observing their bullshit in most of the local Vancouver bars and eateries. Places like The Bombay Bicycle Club, The Hotel Georgia, Hy's Steak House, Le Meridien Lounge, The Four Seasons Lounge, and Chardonnays. Promoters and manipulators frequented all these establishments during the 1980's up to the late 1990's. Since that time period a lot of the establishments have changed names and ownership, probably because so many promoters, who were the best customers, were run out of town by the Securities Commission.

After awhile I got the big picture, I realized the majority of these promoters were just that, bullshit heapers running around mooching a few hundred dollars here and there from brokers and small company management. Then running out and telling each other stories hoping the story would be told down the line and someone would buy one thousand shares so the bullshit artist could run back and claim a tout and ask for another 100 dollars.

Most of the individuals involved in these types of deals still to this day do not have a clue on how to sell anything. They all got involved somehow in the market side or in mineral exploration, got involved with a bunch of other guys with the same amount of knowledge, during a good bull market, their knowledge on how to sell amounting to nothing. Don't forget in the sixties and seventies and eighties there were always speculative mining or high technology deals running, so it didn't take a financial genius to score big on a few or even one deal to claim his or her fame.

Just like the biggest bull market in history running from 1996 to present day. Every bozo that became a financial advisor, investment broker, or order taker during this time period thinks he is, or she is, a financial genius, a boy wonder or girl wonder of investing. Well when the whole world is buying stock, it is not that hard to throw a dart and see any loser deal move higher. That's the rule of supply and demand discussed later on. However, when no one wants to buy stock how do you find someone to buy your deal?

That was my dilemma. I researched most of the deals that existed at the time, hung around, and saw what was happening on the promotion and manipulation side of things. Watched how the promoters were promoting, seeing the fruits of their labors, usually not much. Saw that most of the promoters were trying to sell the same crowd all the deals, and hardly any knew how to sell anything to someone. Only a handful of promoters were leading edge at the time. Most were doing the same lame sell jobs as the others, unsophisticated phone calling of past leads who were laid out on a previous deal long ago and not interested in buying another stock from the lame promoter.

I saw I had good deals but no one knew about them, no one understood what was happening, and no one wanted to buy a stock that just sat waiting for someone to buy it. Real marketing and promotion was required, and along the way an understanding of market psychology, human investing psychology was acquired. With all the promotion and hanging around the losers, I quickly understood you could not do what the losers were doing that was why they were losers. I had to think differently and do things differently to be successful, near the end of my public company career my ad ideas were starting to be copied by many promoters. The cold calling and selling techniques that were already being used by real estate gurus just had to be applied to selling stock.

The first real step to protecting your money is learning what bullshit, scam deal is, and then you progress to understand the more sophisticated scam deals. Learning the basic characteristics of these different types of scam deals will save you many sleepless nights in the future. The stock market's been around for a long time, real smart people have been around for along time, and usually the real smart guys have found out things because they have been in a similar situation as you have, only earlier. The main difference between you and a smart person though is the fact the smart person has learned how to think.

For instance, I thought I was the only guy, the smartest prick to ever walk on the face of the planet, to have figured out the supply and demand theory wasn't some bullshit half baked retarded theory made up by some guy smoking dope or a pipe in his darkened room. I even thought I was smarter when I thought the crappy mess I was in had to be caused by my way of thinking and to now get out of the fucking crappy mess I had to learn to think differently than what got me in this mess to start with.

The supply and demand theory works, and so does changing your way of thinking.

Typical Scam Deal

Having given you a bit of background on my experience, credibility and stock market introduction I'll start with a few descriptions of what typical scams would look like, the factors involved in identifying a scam deal setup. I will focus on mining exploration deals, but also include high tech deals; along the way, I will explain how people who understand how to sell these investments sell them so you can be wary of these techniques. Most of the time, a real con man can sell you anything. He will do this by trying to build up trust between you and himself and use this emotional bond that has been forged to his advantage, to manipulate and control you into buying his manipulation.

Remember not all deals are scams, some are real and I'll explain from my experience what I believe a real deal should look like, but even then those would be manipulated in a sense, as every deal needs some market making until it evolves to a bigger life of it's own, a truly market deal. Market making is basically providing an opportunity for investors to purchase stock in a company by having offers in a market, and also to allow investors the opportunity to sell stock in a company by having bids in a market.

Then I will also outline deals that are just bullshit not a scam but are just full of losers that will never accomplish anything, just continually suck your money dry, and never deliver anything. If you buy these deals, you will not even be able to sell the shit you bought. To make matters worse most times you will end up buying the same losers deal again without knowing it, because they might be involved in many other bogus deals. They will keep selling you because they know you already bought a crappy deal before. You are on the sucker list they hand some phone guy, the voice on the other end of the phone will be different but the person paying the phone bill and selling you the stock is the same as the last deal you got suckered into buying.

Scam Deal Structure

The majority, I would say over 90%, of Canadian stock deals are all similar in structure. The majority of Over The Counter ("OTC") stock deals also follow this structure. I know now you are thinking this person is telling me every deal is bullshit, this person is a nut. One of the two reasons they are all similar in structure is because everyone, promoters, insiders, stockbrokers, lawyers, accountants, continue to structure deals the same way as was done since the 1960's. Most promoters, insiders, stockbrokers, lawyers and accountants today that are involved in controlling a public company all had to start somewhere in the industry. As they progressed through the hierarchy in these public deals either at a particular firm or working for a previous promoter, all the tricks of success, and manipulation, would be passed along to these new people. As the industry grows over time, the number of people slowly being let in on how deals are structured for easy manipulation and how to manipulate grows exponentially.

For this reason, over 90% of the deals follow this scam structure. The second reason over 90% of stock deals follow this structure is the fact the majority of stockbrokers who will sponsor a deal for listing on a Stock Exchange will only sponsor a deal with this structure. In essence, the Industry itself has mandated this particular structure of a deal to gain sponsorship on a Stock Exchange.

The management of a stock deal listed on junior Canadian Stock Exchanges or the even less regulated OTC market in the United States is required to disclose previous employment. Many of these deals could have some management that have previous employment as a bartender or a waiter, or similar unrelated work experiences. In these particular cases if the remainder of the management includes a lawyer and/or an accountant and as long as the deal is structured along the lines of this scam deal structure, there would be a sponsor of the deal for Listing. These management background disclosures are contained in Prospectus' and Offering Memorandums and in Annual General Meeting documents. All these materials for any particular listed deal can be viewed online at the **www.sedar.com**, for Canadian listed companies, and **www.sec.gov**, for USA listed companies. I can provide many past examples of this situation, which really is a truly ludicrous situation. However, even more ludicrous is the fact Joe public would willingly be convinced to purchase a deal with a management background like this even after they are given an offering memorandum and prospectus disclosing this fact. I suspect most investors never read these documents.

Some smart guy, in the 1960's, determined the best structure to manipulate a stock deal with the least amount of money, so everyone copies this structure and operates the same way, the modus operandi you could say. This modus operandi has been used for so long and has been copied by 99% of the individuals involved in the stock market, and yet, until today revealed here in my book, enforcement officials do not know this fact.

The structure of the company would be low capital. Anywhere from 1.5 million to under 20 million shares issued. Many of the initial shares in friendly hands, lets term them insider shares. It would be disclosed within the prospectus or Annual General meeting documents that anywhere from 20% or more shares of the outstanding amount would constitute this insider share position. In many cases, these insider shares were obtained by paying hardly any consideration, and in numerous situations paying absolutely no consideration. Just to clarify this for you I will explain it better. No money is paid for the shares. This last fact is difficult to prove in most instances if no real thorough Forensic Audit is done, but from all my experiences from dealing with many of the promoters, this is a prevalent situation.

Then the minimum share distribution through an initial public offering (IPO) is completed to the minimum required individuals with insiders, who could be promoters, directors, and stockbrokers, taking the majority of the deal. These IPO's must be distributed to the public but in the major jurisdictions of British Columbia, Alberta Quebec, and Ontario, there are minimum amounts of the IPO to be distributed to a minimum number of public shareholders. This is true also for all major jurisdictions in the United States of America and in Europe. During the IPO boom of the bull market since 1996, the majority of IPO's even on NASDAQ or NYSE would have been sold to the minimum amount of investors with enough promotion being done so that the public would help drive the stock higher in frenzied trading. The institutions doing the IPO and company insiders would take the majority of the IPO and then sell it higher into the frenzied trading. There are in most cases rules and regulations on the amount of stock that insiders and brokerage sponsors are allowed to purchase of an IPO but these rules and regulations are always skirted.

I witnessed this same situation with a few IPO's on the Milan stock exchange in Italy. The shares had minimal distribution; the whole of Italy knew the stocks were going to be listed to trade and on trading they were driven up 3 times the IPO price. Huge trading ensued, after a few months the stocks settled back below the IPO price. The same manipulation techniques I am describing were used even in far off Italy. Please note I was not involved in any of these deals.

The sponsoring broker theoretically will have the distribution setup but will very rarely supply most of the general public clients. In 95% of the cases, I am now referring to the typical Canadian deal, the promoters of the deal help find individuals who would participate in the offering, unless the broker dealers lead broker is directly involved in the deal. In this scenario, the broker dealer supplies most of the IPO clients, and they retain the majority of the IPO, and then sell the IPO after stock listing into the market. They will ensure that the IPO is well sought after and will let more affluent individuals who are in the industry get a few more shares than the public, because they know these people will talk up the stock that much more, so that they themselves can unload the stock. This is described later in the IPO financings chapter. This trick was used prevalently during the recent 1996 bull market.

The main reason for the promoter to finance his own deal is the fact there could be at times over 5000 of these deals listed on the junior or OTC market, and most people end up buying the bogus or scam deals in the after market. The aftermarket is the public trading market once the IPO has been distributed and the stock has started trading. Any stock that has been trading since yesterday and you purchase today you are purchasing stock in the after market.

The majority of people who are drawn to these types of speculative deals have bought prior deals in the aftermarket. In most cases, they have money tied up in these prior deals. Due to the scam deal situation, investors are not able to sell their positions. Usually investors are unable to sell due to the psychological factors of price levels and investor naivety. In this case, stockbrokers cannot approach these individuals to buy any of the stock of an IPO. The majority of the clients have been stuck in the prior bogus deals and never made any money to reinvest. The Promoter then has individuals to put up the minimum amount money for the minimum amount of stock. When the IPO begins trading in the aftermarket, the individuals who bought the small amount of IPO are usually the first to buy additional stock in the aftermarket. As they have been hyped by the broker or promoter to buy rather than sell.

Another factor is the broker receives a commission for the IPO and the less amount of work the better, unless he has a direct investment in the deal. In all jurisdictions, a broker is not allowed to have an interest in the deal he is listing, unless the interest is disclosed, and then limitations are placed on the selling of this stock. This information is discussed in some more detail in the same chapter as the IPO financings.

Once the IPO is completed and the aftermarket begins then of course with a low issued share capital, most deals will sit and not trade, or will be manipulated to a higher level, at each moment, the manipulator waits for a victim to bid for the stock or buy the offer. In either scenario, typically, these deals will have small offers so that if it is bought it is easier to have the price move forward. It is important to note that many of these factors involved in a market manipulation avoid the general rule of supply and demand, but do in the end become a victim of the rule of supply and demand.

The theory of this typical scam deal structure is of course with the low capital, the low number of shares issued, and the low number of shares working against a promoter or group of promoters there is less money required by a manipulator to move a stock to a higher price giving the appearance of value. The less sophisticated manipulators will then begin touting everyone they know in the industry or individuals that they have previously sold similar past deals to. This usually results in the same disastrous return for the unsuspecting individuals, buying high priced no value stock that crumbles after the manipulator has let the price fall because there is no underlying support by the general public once the manipulators bids disappear.

In a nut shell, the theory does not work for a number of reasons, in the majority of cases, mainly because as the higher the price goes the greedier the manipulators are, they eventually forget to sell, or do sell, but have higher prices now, and this translates to higher priced bids. When a seller not involved in the manipulation sells shares, even a small number, at the higher price, most times the manipulators buy. Eventually they are buying at higher prices giving themselves bigger headaches, because in reality it is harder to get people to buy low capital high priced stock.

Most times the local individuals, stock promoters, stockbrokers, market players, involved in the local stock market, knowing the track record of the manipulator(s) involved, don't even bother buying the stock and the manipulator ends up buying back most of the stock himself at the higher levels. Not being able to run the deal, and having the deal languish because of this typical Canadian deal structure will always have the stock tank to low prices with minimal trading. The price retreats so far that the amount of trading becomes next to nothing on a daily basis.

Always the price will tank to low levels with this share structure. If the promoter is successful in raising the stock price to offload his position, the stock will eventually fall back since no underlying asset is present to support a stock price. If the promoter cannot offload his position but has raised the price, the stock will collapse also. It will collapse because in most cases, the promoter will move the price too high and investors with stock will want to sell the stock to get out of it. With this scenario to move the price higher, the promoter would be bidding. With others selling and the promoter buying, he will buy back too many shares and the stock will tank. The share structure is not appealing to investors because most investors want to trade large cap, large trading volume stocks. The recent increase in day trading has resulted in this phenomenon of trading high capitalized stocks with large daily trading volumes so as to be able to unload the position fast to protect yourself.

The more sophisticated manipulators will promote the company to the unsuspecting public. They will usually do this by trying to attach themselves to a successful deal. In mining deals, junior miners will acquire exploration ground near a successful project. This is a good idea as past discoveries show that sometimes the same discovery extends onto adjoining ground. It would be a good deal if the individuals have a good exploration track record or really do spend money on the exploration because anything could happen in regards to good results in very good geology, but if the management has no track record, you are just giving your money away.

The management would have this share structured deal and would manipulate the shares to a high price. One trick of manipulating the shares is to have bids and offers in uniform size and uniform price intervals. For example, bids could be stacked with size of 5,000 shares or in even increments of 5,000 or 10,000 shares, or higher amounts.

These bids would be placed at each 5 cent interval below the market price. Likewise offers of 5,000 shares, or another uniform amount of stock, would be stacked again in increments of 5 cents above the market price. Bid refers to the price an individual wants to buy stock at, offer, refers to the price an individual wants to sell stock at. The ask price is a term that also refers to the offer.

This is the typical scenario played out 100% of the time. The market visible, shown in the newspaper or on a computer screen to the potential investor is the bid and ask, but the more sophisticated investors can look to see the underlying bids below, and the offers above the market price. The market price is the price at which stock is trading. This is done through trading accounts online, or paying for a service that offers market trading or supplies stock ticker information, these days the majority of brokerage services or stock information services offer this market depth feature through online services.

To encourage individuals to buy, the manipulator has these bids and offers outside of the market to give the appearance of a true market. In simple terms, the bids and offers a more sophisticated investor can see below the bid and above the offer of a trading stock are stacked in a uniform fashion.

The question you have to ask yourself is how in this world can there be a uniform market for a stock below the bid and above the offer? It is really a silly premise to begin with. The manipulator is trying to show underlying price support for the stock and offers for the stock hoping someone possibly a trader who has a large order for stock will place the order and take out offers above the current offer to fill his demand. Avoid these deals immediately.

A true trading stock will be trading in and around the market price. There will be big bids and big offers at the trading price. Rarely will there be any stacked bids and offers outside of the trading price. The practice of uniform bids and offers rarely occurs in a real trading situation.

Big bids and big offers usually mean good liquidity and are the main factor of a real legitimate market, however these three features, big bids, big offers and good liquidity, of a truly public market can be manipulated disclosed further in the book.

If there are no offers on a stock or small sized offers, the bait is there to get the public to move the price higher. Avoid these deals. The price could swing up 15 cents on a legitimate buy but when an investor wishes to sell the stock, the price will be at much, much lower levels. Additionally, after the legitimate buy, the stock will again revert back to the original bid and ask, or be moved up with small bid sizes, 500 shares or 1,000 shares since the manipulator will be afraid to buy the stock he just sold, or sold previously.

This is an example of what I have described.

Assume stock symbol XXXX trades on the TSX and the bid price of $0.45, with additional bids visible through a market depth program of $0.40, $0.35, $0.30, $0.25, $0.20, with bid sizes of 5,000 shares at each price point. The offer price of $0.50 and additional higher offers of $0.55, $0.60, $0.65, and $0.70 all with offer size of 5,000 are also visible through the market depth option.

The bid and offer for the stock symbol XXXX is $0.45–$0.50. The bids below, and the offers above the "manipulated market" price are set, giving the appearance through the tool of market depth that a demand for the stock exists, and a ready supply even though small is available at higher prices.

The small size offers are again a symptom of the Canadian structured deal, the premise being that other seasoned veterans can see stock is available to buy, but a minimal amount so the stock has to be tightly held.

The manipulator or a phone monkey or phone chimp, both terms referring to telemarketers, will use the following type of promotional lines to try and get an investor similar to yourself to buy stock in this type of deal. "The stock is a tightly held stock, hardly any on the offer. It won't take much to move this stock higher." Avoid any deal where this type of talk occurs. If talk of price moving higher in the following weeks is used, avoid this deal also, how in this world can anyone predict the future?

Promotional Methods, Mail outs, Boiler Rooms

Once the manipulator has a project, they will promote the company. They will do this by placing advertisements in industry specific magazines or newspapers. Or, advertise in financial newspapers or magazines, or even on the Internet. One or all of these avenues of generating warm leads could take place. There are industry specific promoting avenues on the Internet or in hard copy that target individuals who buy speculative stocks. Additionally, there are also avenues of promoting to industry specific or stock sector specific groups of investors. There are also newsletter writers and Investment analysts who will tout a company for a fee or even for stock. Usually the stock is given free. There is a section in the book further on about this topic.

A warm lead is the easiest sell if you know how to sell. When an individual answers an ad, the individual is showing the interest level in the offering in the ad and is showing the fact money is ready to buy. At my peak, I was able to convert 100% of warm leads, and I would use different techniques to sell, the soft sell, the hard sell, and the abusive sell. I will describe these techniques in some detail in a later chapter.

Mailing Lists

Mailing lists can be bought and sold all the time. Individuals would be on a few if they bought a prior deal or have a brokerage account. With these lists, targeted mail outs can be done, or email blasts today with Internet email lists being bought and sold. With hard follow up sales calls, any stock can be sold to a warm lead. If the phone person knows how to sell stock, stock is a hard sell as it is selling a dream, and because it is a piece of paper and nothing really tangible, it is the hardest sell to make, unless there is a huge bull market, then any stock can be sold. Most times the typical Canadian share structure deal will collapse before this step because with over 60% of the deals structured like this, the majority of manipulators do not have selling techniques.

Boiler Rooms

Boiler rooms can be employed by a listed company from either boiler room operators, or used by the listed company manipulators themselves. In essence the majority of scam deals will have their own phone center within the office or offsite, most times the phones are manned by the manipulators in other cases where large operations are conducted, phone monkeys or phone chimps are utilized, both terms refer to telemarketers. In simplest terms, these phone monkeys or chimps will call the mailing or phone lists or individuals who are known to buy stock deals.

The concept of cold calling or learning how to find new clients has waned over the years as periodic visits by the author to a large number of public company offices suggests the majority of individuals rely on the old habits formed from working for or with earlier manipulators.

New concepts of selling have hardly been employed in Canada, because the imagination of selling is not present in the groups of promoters left. Movies like Boiler Room are true to form, as these concepts of selling have evolved in the United States. The techniques of cold calling investors works, and I would suggest watching a movie like Boiler Room, because from my own experience the general premise of the movie is a legitimate view of real life, there are hokey points and moments, but once an individual becomes comfortable on the phone they can sell anyone anything.

In my early years, I would venture to New York and New Jersey to find promoters to promote my deals, or investors to buy stock in my deals. On one particular occasion, I ran into an individual named Barry Davis. He was touted to me by a local promoter/manipulator who had used Barry Davis to promote a few of his stock listings. Davis' operation was in New Jersey, back in the mid 1980's. He even had an 800 number and a 900 number you could call to get his stock tip of the day. He had a huge operation.

I dropped in unannounced back then and could not believe what I saw. Davis had the ground floor of a tower, with shades drawn, fully occupied. In walking into the first floor office, the first thing noticed were rows, and rows of tables. The tables all had phones, and a multitude of people. The phone people consisted of African-American, Irish, Italian, Jewish, and East Indian heritage, both men and women, old and young. It was non stop phone calling. Davis had all the phones hooked up to a computer running a telemarketing program that allowed Davis or any of his other two cronies to listen in on any conversation. Davis was a Jew and I doubt that was his real last name. When I entered, no one stopped what he or she was doing. Davis was wide eyed for a second then he hit sell mode, a machine gun mouth trying to size me up and weasel anything he could out of me. My eyes were wide open soaking all this up. It was quite unbelievable.

Davis' office was in the back and one of his cohorts; an older woman was watching us, while another weasel was on an earpiece listening in on a particular phone call. An African-American kid came in during our meeting to tell them he thought he had a Securities and Exchange investigator on the line. This kid was certain it was someone who had called before but had given a different name on the previous call. This had Davis and the other two in the room go into, I would call it, skin saving mode. The portly guy on the earpiece switched to the kid's channel, Davis told him some lines to use, and the kid went off.

When this was happening I took the opportunity to survey the room we were in. I quickly scanned over the crap on his desk, on the shelves, and in the trashcan. I noticed a ton of brochures on a few local Vancouver deals, and saw a large amount of business cards in the trashcan. They were G.M.'s business cards. G was a well known, and distinguished stockbroker in Vancouver. G.M. was very successful and was distinguished through his community involvement and service. He was at the top of the game in Vancouver in the late 80's even though his brokerage firm had been implicated in a number of big stock fraud cases. A few months after my New Jersey visit G passed away; he of course had made millions on the typical deal share structure. I presume Davis was promoting some of his deals in the United States.

Davis was a bullshitter, and a guy like me showing up was like red riding hood visiting the wolf in grandma's clothes. He wanted my stock so he could blast it out at me; my deal at the time was trading at around $2.00 a share. His bullshit was even better than what I had heard in my first encounters with promoters on Howe Street in Vancouver. This was New York, bigger and better in everyway. I left without any dealings with Davis. As I left, he was barking after me, calling me names because I did not go for his crap. Reminded me of when I was a kid, and people would call you names when they did not get what they wanted.

Davis' operation was closed a few months or weeks later, the FBI and SEC closed down his operation. He was a real bad guy, always wondered though why all the people from Vancouver were not implicated in any of the scams.

The Business of Promoting

If the project is in a good area, then a lot of times a few local brokers will become involved in the deal and work with a promoter. This becomes a promotional group who of course have the same idea in mind of manipulating the stock, and promoting it to higher levels to unload cheap stock or stock that was acquired by paying no consideration. The brokers will be selling to individual clients. Remember the more brains working on the deal the more touting. Usually though someone in the group will be back dooring the deal because he knows the underlying scam and he will be selling his paper to the others first. Back dooring is giving the appearance of playing along with the group of manipulators but all the while working in your own best interests.

Once the manipulator has his advertising program, and/or mailing program he will start to manipulate the stock, to bring in the people who might be looking at the stock price due to the promotional campaign.

With the structure of the deals being low capital the price is moved higher and unsuspecting individuals who have over a time period been watching the stock moving up continuously will of course not want to miss out on the opportunity and eventually get sucked into buying the stock.

The soft sell employed would be used as a way of getting you to buy; this technique would be employed in the following typical manner. An out of town potential investor will call unexpectedly on the stock and enquire about the stock and its projects or potential. The facts would be given on the company focusing on the area that is being promoted, the project or whatever the angle is. The investor would be sold on the no hard sell technique, the facts being put forward, with a ho hum attitude by the soft seller. This soft sell method allows the investor to decide for his or herself on whether they will invest in the stock or not. In the majority of cases, the soft sell method would convert the potential investor into an investor. This soft sell would work mainly because the investor would have phoned other promoters about other deals and would have been bombarded with hard selling methods or bad selling techniques.

The hard sell technique would be implemented, and would be successful, when a potential investor would email or leave a message or respond to an ad. The hard sell would again point out the facts of the projects but would be presented in a bit harsher or ruder attitude. This cavalier and rude attitude would be employed because the majority of people seem to like to be abused by a stock promoter before they will buy stock in the deal the promoter is promoting. It is human psychology and human behavior that I witnessed first hand. The more I abused a potential investor the more they were willing to buy stock. I would be able to convert 100% of potential investors emailing, calling, or responding to an ad.

The abusive sell always was employed with someone calling up locally who already owned stock or a professional locally involved in the market. The usual reply to a question immediately was I do not know, and eventually in the conversation, reference would be made to just sell the fucking crappy stock, and, who the fuck told you or your client to buy the fucking stock in the first place. Leave the fucking stock alone. This type of attitude and abusive selling would always convert the caller into a buyer. The majority of the time when an invested stockholder or a stock professional with a client owning stock, call the promoter or company for information this always translates to the investor or investors adviser wanting to sell the stock. The caller is calling to confirm their desire to sell the stock, nothing else simply to confirm their desire to sell the stock. By not revealing any information, or not knowing any reason for the stock rising or dropping, there is some doubt placed in the investor or investor advisors mind. Being abusive throws the person off. It is an unpredictable behavior pattern that confuses the individual into believing something is up. The confused investor is transferred into thinking either the promoter does not know what is happening, or the promoter wants me to sell. With the investor thinking along these lines, they will instead buy additional stock. Eventually I became so good at the technique that I would convert 100% of the time.

The Pump and Dump

The usual modus operandi of the pump and dump is along the lines noted earlier. Low capital, majority of stock owned by a core group, price moving higher on low trading volumes, with large amounts of money spent on promotion and advertising, usually these costs are hidden in the Financial Statements under administrative costs.

The pump and dump can be utilized with high cap large volume trading stocks also, very easily as long as the group has stock to sell, and has some buying power to help move the price.

With an audience watching the stock, and perhaps the help of one or more stockbrokers showing volume in the deal, many people can be stampeded to buy the stock. The volume in the deal can be created/shown by the same group by buying and selling their own stock at offer prices or bid prices, accounting wise they would only be paying the trade commissions. Just as quickly as the stock has moved to the higher inflated price, once the core group has pulled bids on the stock, and no real market for the deal exists, the stock price will evaporate to previous levels or worse.

There will be unusually high trading volumes, compared to prior trading activity, moving the price higher, once the sell off or dump occurs, the price retreats to the same level. The dump occurs in the elevated trading volume. This scenario never ever attracts the attention of enforcement. Even when an individual investor would file a complaint to draw attention to a particular deal or the insiders involved. The view of most enforcement officials in the Canadian Securities Commissions is that any individual who wanted to make quick money deserves what has happened to the price of the get rich quick stock. There will be no sympathy for you or the money you have lost. To them you are no better than the manipulator who moved the price and dumped the stock.

This can occur many times in the life of the same stock. The individuals involved will at each lower level stock up again via either private placement, warrant exercising or receiving shares for debt. A private placement is a financing after the IPO that is a financing between the company and an investor or a group of investors amount of shares and the price of the shares will vary. Warrants exercised refers to shares that are converted from warrants at a set price. Warrants are usually issued when a private placement has been completed and each warrant or a number of warrants are exercisable at a share price for a share, this ratio, number of warrants and exercise price vary. Shares for debt refers to shares being issued for debt that has been incurred but not paid with monies.

They then do another pump and dump, to a lower level than any previous highs attained, and suck more money in. The next run up will be to a lower level as a wall will be hit where the individuals cannot sell anymore of their stock but rather the general public who had bought previously on other runs starts to sell into the market, this "wall price" is easily defined as offers and selling appears from everywhere. After a few runs of the pump and dump, which could take a time period of a few years, the core group will do a roll back of the stock, again having a real low capital, then refinancing the company through private placements or shares for debt to get more shares in their hands.

Let me explain the above scenarios. To give you an example of what I am talking about. I will include in here again, a real trading stock company, name not publicized to show you what I am talking about, real time.

Stock trading on the TSX, I will call it, song and dance limited, trading under the improvised symbol of sonda. The company originally was called dance and song limited and over a few years since the listing, the stock had an initial run to $0.50 a share then settled back to $0.10 a share. Nothing happened in the company, the insiders continually would complete private placements for minimal amounts of money to help pay the bills. The bull market starts in 1996 and the stock runs to $8.00 to the bewilderment of the insiders. As the price is moving higher, the insiders continue to fill bids. At the $8.00 price the stock cannot move higher it has reached the reversal point unbeknownst to the insiders.

The insiders then end up bidding for stock to keep the price at this level and have offers to sell stock hoping that more stock can be sold and believing their deal to be worth the lofty $8.00 per share figure when in actual fact there are no tangible assets in the company. The big brex scam is unveiled in early 1997, and the insiders do not pull their bids on their dance and song limited. Over the course of a few weeks the price of dance and song retreats to new lows at each level the insider is putting up bids to secure a price level and offers stock thinking the selling will blow over and buyers will pay higher prices. The stock ends up moving to under $0.10. Every junior exploration deal is hammered this same way during this time period as all insiders of companies did not clue in that brex shone a poor light on the whole industry. How is any investor going to believe anyone in the industry as a whole if none of the experts whose deals they are investing in blew the whistle on brex?

The insider gets smart then starts taking down private placements and washing money in and out at the lower $0.10 to $0.15 range to average his cost back down. The insider inflates fees he is charging for work done on behalf of the dance and song thus being able to take down larger amounts of stock in private placements. With high tech deals in vogue, in 1999 he digs up a small minor tech deal and starts talking about bringing in the deal as a reverse takeover. The stock is then pumped up higher over a four month period and sold off as high as $0.90 a share. This time he does not bid for the stock and fills bids all the way down to $0.10 a share. At this level he refinances via private placement and six months later he pumps the deal to $0.50, again selling and pulling bids to let the deal now drop to less than $0.05 a share.

After a few months the deal is rolled back to form song and dance limited with shares for debt added. The stock sits at mere pennies and some small amounts trade to unsuspecting bidders.

From the beginning of 2002 when the new song and dance has been listed, there have been over 5 million shares in private placement done and over two million shares in director's options set. It is obvious that there is a lot of money washing in and out occurring and insiders loading up on stock. In early May the stock is moved from $0.06 to over $0.30 during a six week period, then from the over $0.30 level a drop down to $0.12 over a four week period.

This my reader is a real case scenario being played out as you read. It is predictable and it follows the modus operandi I have laid out.

Additional examples, especially technical charts of company's that were known manipulations can be found on my website, **www.marinospecogna.com**. These charts are very self explanatory as the manipulated deal charts can be used to superimpose over a present day deal to see if the charts follow similar patterns.

The rollback always results in the individual shareholders break even price that much higher. It also results in the stock having no tradable value and just having the individual innocent investor stuck in the deal forever. This is all great for the manipulator as the stuck investor continues to be a part of the core shareholder base. What is so ironic of course is that even though in the rollback the public ends up with hardly any large overall total number of shares compared to the new outstanding share figure. The roll back also ensures the company receives a new name. Making it that much harder for a shareholder to follow the new stock. Coincidentally the insider group will complete after rollback private financings to augment their position. Then the core group goes through and completes more pump and dumps. They have you sucked in as a shareholder and will meet any exchanges minimum shareholder requirements with all the old shareholders left with their now fraction of a shareholding, and at the same time they, the insiders, have the majority of the issued stock in the new company.

Rollbacks are bad business dealings, and I would suggest they are indicative of a market manipulation. As I am writing, much is being made of NORTEL, and NORTEL's proposed rollback. I will give you my take on NORTEL further on.

Management Credibility

In this scenario of rollbacks and pump and dumps, the typical management of these deals will be individuals who are on the board of a number of companies. In most cases the other deals would all have the same modus operandi. The individuals in a majority of the cases will be administrative groups, lawyers and accountants. These groups do not expend money directly in either junior mining exploration or in research and development of a high tech deal. Money not expended in exploration or research and development will ensure the deal fails. The money usually raised or incurred in debt is spent on administrative fees going directly to the individual. When shares are issued for debt, the insider is receiving the shares. The individuals will be directors of a number of deals and in most cases will even have all the deals run out of the same office.

In all the past deals and companies these individuals would have been involved with no track record of successful project completion can ever be found. They have no record of accomplishment of a mineral discovery or no record of producing a product or no record of completing a new research discovery or a high tech positive result. Their promotional capabilities and promoting factor is their supposed experience of being involved in other deals, past deals, using the concept since someone has been involved in an industry for over 10 years or 20 years, whatever that number may be, that for the longevity to have occurred they must have some experience. In reality the deals never provided any tangible assets, any real discovery, or earnings, just stock price fluctuations, increases and decreases, that kept sucking hard earned money from individual investors.

In Review Important Factors and Tricks To Watch For

A very important factor to remember is in any scam deal is the fact there will be a minor amount of bids and a minor amount of offers, in combination with small bid size and small offer size. The minor offers, and small offer size, allows for sudden price increases. This is because a small amount of shares are available for sale allowing the opportunity to move the price higher at any time a reasonable sized buy order is placed at market price. The small bid sizes save the manipulator from buying unwanted stock. With the stacked bid prices being manipulators bids, the low number of bids and small size of bids means that if a large sell order occurs the manipulator won't be too exposed to buying too much of this third party stock. If the third party, Joe Public, put in a market sell order the amount of money to be shelled out by the promoter would be minimal.

In researching a company, a speculative venture, look for issued capital size; look at daily trading volumes, managements background, and experience, and the number of different company's the directors are involved in or have been involved in. Factors to determine while watching the stock trade or just sit idle for a few days are these. What happens to price when volume trades, do 10,000 shares move the price of the stock up 10 cents or higher? Does 10,000 shares of sudden selling drop the price 10 cents or more? How many other deals are the Directors involved in? Who are the directors, have they ever made a significant discovery, or been in a successful enterprise, venture or buyout? Is the stock trading at a very high price, with not much daily share volume? What do the Financial Statements look like? Are the majority of the company's funds being spent on administrative costs? Who brought the company to your attention?

Many of these facts can be researched on the Internet through different sites. For Canada the SEDAR site at **www.sedar.com**, will give you all the filings a public company has made, from the information provided you can look at Annual and Quarterly Financial Statements, and other director information, as well as Insider Trading Reports. You can view stock prices from a number of websites, with past historical prices and volumes provided. In the United States, the Securities and Exchange Commission has an incredible site with all available company information. The web address is **www.sec.gov**.

On research look at share capital, low capital combined with low price, should be viewed as a bad sign. Avoid a deal, where past shares for debt have occurred. Avoid a deal, where share roll backs (consolidations) occurred in the past.

It is important to note if the same management was involved in these cases, and whether the same management had been involved in shares for debt or roll backs with other deals they are involved with.

Analyze trading volume, particularly whether there is any. Do more than 10,000 shares trade a day, does the deal trade everyday. As an investor you need the shares to trade everyday, you need volume, and you need negligible price increases.

Of course if the deal is trading huge volumes, over 100,000 shares and trading at a very low price, and the other conditions of managements past history are seen to be those of rollbacks or shares for debt then leave that deal alone. The modus operandi is there and the volumes will be pulling you in, sooner than later that deal will be rolled back also.

In some very real cases occurring today, trading volumes of hundred of thousands of shares, and millions of shares could be occurring. Big volume, negligible price increases but management track records that stink, so avoid these deals.

On stock trading analysis, is one specific brokerage selling more than all the others combined, this will show you this particular brokerage firm has an account off loading stock. Most manipulators are not sophisticated enough to use jitney trading of large amounts of stock to hide selling.

I found traders, day traders; look for certain signs in an active trading stock. Good high cap deals, with good trading volumes over 100,000 shares a day with a large number of trades, fluctuating from 5–10 cents a day, sometimes 15 cents a day attract trading and day trader attention. This trading activity will lure traders as it shows liquidity and price movement two signs for traders to jump into the mix. Another trick to provide a huge number of trades a day is to jitney trade stock through houses that have recently bought stock to show even trading. Jitney trading is selling stock from one brokerage house through another brokerage house so there appears more brokerage house following.

There are trading systems that will allow you to type a day range of trading for a stock to show you the brokerage houses buying and selling stock and the average price. Of course, if a professional watches this they will be alarmed to see one or two houses outright selling more than buying stock. The reason is of course there is unloading, dumping happening. The trick is then to mask the selling by jitneying through houses that recently bought stock. Most traders will of course buy to sell but if the stock keeps trading between good levels, more traders get attracted and the price can be manipulated at a certain price level if shares are available to sell. The manipulator at the top of the game will ensure there is ample stock to sell. Masking the selling is the trick and the jitney method is the preferred method as well as use of nominee accounts and offshore nominee accounts.

Applying the Factors to a Real Time Trading Deal

A good example of a high cap deal with a few factors present would be NORTEL.

Large trading volumes with a number of individual trades a day and not major price fluctuations would suggest a real market deal. Of course in these deals also, there will be professional traders playing the volume so prices would fluctuate 5 to 10 cents a day, but there wouldn't be a huge price run up over a short period of time unless of course something significant would be happening.

Again in this case the usual modus operandi would not be present, as the share capital would have to be large; a minimum "floor level" of over 10 million shares issued and widely distributed, in this case the shares would be distributed widely enough that a real demand for the stock exists. Again, trading volume has to be compared to shares issued. If both are high, the chances of being scammed are minimal. However, the price has to be a reasonable price.

I think, from all my personal experiences where there is a lack of major developments or projects being undertaken but volume is high in the deal. The floor level at the minimum or higher, meaning over 10 million shares issued. I believe the price should still be well under the $0.50 a share level or there might be a manipulation occurring.

If the price is higher, there could still be a manipulation happening. Again this theory works, look at NORTEL, at the time of writing this, NORTEL had tanked to under $1.00 Canadian on phenomenal volumes, but a true market has developed for the paper. Huge trading volumes with nice price runs have occurred. At the editing stage of this book, the Nortel stock has now rebounded to over $3.00 per share with huge, tens of millions of shares a day trading.

In summary, the factors of a typical scam deal would be this: a small capital share structure, management with no relative experience, management diluted between a number of company's, managements prior history of shares for debt and roll backs, low trading volumes, minimal bids, minimal offers, large price fluctuations upwards on minimal volume or swings downwards on minimal volume. Scam deals can also be high priced with low share capital, high capitalization and high priced, high cap and low priced with large daily trading volumes, dependent on the other factors being present.

Very Bad Scenario

In the United States Over the counter market ("OTC"), the other problem that exists for an investor is the fact that with less regulation and the rules applicable to this market, any individual involved in a listed company on the OTC can also be the share transfer agent for the particular company. A share transfer company is the company that issues new share capital of the listed company and keeps the shareholders list for the listed company. Any stock of the listed company that is transferred, bought, or sold must be submitted by clearing agencies to the Transfer Agent for registration of the new shareholders name. Stock does not have to be registered in the new purchasers name unless requested by the new purchaser.

On regulated exchanges in Canada and the United States other than the OTC and the Pink sheet market, companies are required by rules and regulations to have a separate share transfer company, usually a bank or a trust company, to administer the issuance of new shares, upon regulatory approval, and to administer the company's shareholder roster.

The OTC and pink sheeted companies not inter listed on another exchange do not have the share transfer company rule or regulation nor do share issuances have to be approved by a regulatory agency. A company could issue its own new shares any time, and this will happen countless times, and in this way there maybe 10 million shares stated as issued when in fact the company has over 50 million shares issued, the insiders having continually created new shares and sold them immediately

On regulated exchanges, the fact that Regulatory Agencies have not devised a proper structure to track share issuances by Share Transfer Agents is a bad factor. In most cases a very regulated Exchange will only require a Listed Company and an individual to sign an undertaking that they will not sell stock they have bought in a private placement before the time required by Rules and Regulations. There is an assurance made that no stock will be sold before the hold period. This is usually not followed. There is no Regulation requiring the Stock Transfer Agent to post a Legend on the stock, the regulations call for the Company and individuals subscribing to private placement stock to ask for a Legend. A Legend on a stock certificate is simply a bold faced stamped note that this particular share certificate cannot be sold or transferred before a specific date. Most manipulators worth anything will not ask for these Legends.

Be Wary Of Private Placements

This fact of no requirement for Legends to be placed on Stock Certificates is a major factor. This allows manipulators to conduct private placements in a particular stock and allows them to immediately, once Regulatory approval has occurred, to obtain the shares that have been subscribed for and sell these shares into the unsuspecting market. A similar trick is for a Broker Sponsored secondary offering to be suddenly approved by Regulatory Agencies without prior notice, the price of the Offering priced well below the current market price. In some cases, the Brokered Offerings may be announced. Brokered Offerings allow for the stock to be sold immediately, if the stock is trading at premium to what the subscription price is that stock is sold or has been previously short sold, or just sold previously with brokerage house approval, as documents would have been used to confirm future delivery of the stock.

Any sort of financing can be the manipulators way of reloading on stock to sell into the market, without a doubt that is what occurs the majority of the time.

NORTEL

NORTEL is discussed as it has come to the forefront as I am writing this book. NORTEL and many, many others are classic examples of the fraud or manipulated deal dressed up to take advantage of investors in a bull market.

As an example, let us start at the end of NORTEL, today. The facts known up until today, September 30, 2002, are these. The CEO has publicly announced that NORTEL has a huge cash position and a huge debt facility which he will not take advantage of. The stock is trading below $0.80 a share Canadian with huge daily volume of over 60 million shares a day on both the Toronto and New York Stock Exchanges, this fact leads well into the next chapter on supply and demand. This huge volume suggests sellers and buyers, legitimate real sellers and buyers; the low price suggests a real market.

The problem is this, for NORTEL to keep its New York listing it is required to trade over $1.00US per share. The sticking point is NORTEL has over 3.4 billion shares issued and has low earnings, not to mention the fact it does not pay a dividend. What it also has is over $2 billion in cash and cash equivalents. Not all money can be in cash, it has to be invested, and those are called equivalents. It has reported over 25% less earnings are expected in the quarter to end soon.

Earlier in the year, as the stock price was tanking, a financing was completed for almost 1 billion shares at under $1.00 per share. Insiders were touted as buying stock, with reporters in Canada towing the promoted hype to them, of insiders believing the company will turn around. When I first read this story on the financing, and the precipitous fall of the market with the huge volumes I shook my head and laughed.

Two real scenarios most likely had been played out. First you have to ask yourself, why would anyone want to finance a collapsing deal, remember NORTEL was trading at huge prices, it hit over $120/share at one time, and now it was crapping out big time.

I would say the two scenarios read like this. First, the majority of the brokers financing the deal, and insiders, may have been shorting the stock on the way down, and now were covering the shorts with fresh new paper. They could have sold short the full 1 billion shares at higher prices and were covering the shorts with the new financing. The difference in the price they sold at and now paid for the stock would represent their profit. Short selling is borrowing stock from another broker whose client owns the stock and selling it to a buyer. Rules specify that the shares be sold at a higher price than the last trade, so they would have to be offered for sale not immediately sold off into the market. There are margin requirements, for selling short, you are required to post additional money as margin collateral incase the shares move higher then the brokerage firm will step in and buy the amount of shares you have sold short.

The second scenario is the individuals involved were reloading to sell more paper without pre shorting, perhaps having created cash earlier by converting stock for cash by selling into the public shares previously bought or exercising directors options. A billion shares financing at $1.00 per share is a billion dollars. That money goes into the company's treasury and the stock goes to the people who bought the financing. When the stock was running up through manipulation, the low price and (with big brokers involved), big money to play the deal, trading the stock, the offers could be gobbled easily. The bids moved higher, would draw in unsuspecting individuals. The fact the financial news papers were doped into writing the story of "insiders are buying because they believe in the company's future", would have sucked huge amounts of Joe public money into the deal.

Remember 1 billion shares at $1.00 per share equal $1 billion dollars. Now if the stock is sold even $0.50 more, that is a profit of $500 million. I believe without looking at the chart that the stock traded well over that amount of shares over a time, and the market demand would have sucked that amount of stock quite easily over a short time.

I believe that a version of both scenarios could have taken place. Most likely, the majority of the stock was short sold as the price was falling from the highs of 52 weeks ago, from $7.50 to the financing price range. The short sold stock was then covered with a part of the financing and a large amount of shares were bought from the profit being the price the shares were short sold at and the financing price level of these shares. The new shares acquired would be fed now again to the unsuspecting public with the huge trading volumes being generated in the stock.

The current Nortel prices and trading volumes would be a true price, a true supply and demand price.

Watch the shorts on the deal then pay attention to announced financings, I would suspect that as the individuals find they are successful, make a large amount of easy money the first time, they will commit the same scenario repeated. Having shorted x amount of stock, they subscribe for x plus y amount of stock, the x amount of stock covering the short position and y amount of stock being the new created share position. This allows the individuals to follow the scenario previously laid out of the Canadian Share Structure.

The NORTEL rumored rollback will cut the amount of shares in the publics hands, with the premise the price will be now the same amount as the rollback, 30 for 1 would see a price 30 times more. In reality, the price if it trades at 30 times more is really the same price as before consolidation. However, as this technique is one described earlier, the stock will actually tank more. Most likely, after the rollback or, just before, a new financing will be reported, again to cover the shorts accumulated in the wild huge volumes currently trading, and repositioning to sell additional shares. Further rollbacks would occur, if this scenario becomes played out.

NORTEL is a classic example of a manipulated deal. Do not scoff, look at the track record, and re-read above. NORTEL has huge sales because it was created as a monopoly, it will have earnings, and it has large cash reserves because of the huge amounts of money raised, even most recently. It lacks the one factor that makes a major blue chip a legitimate deal and that is dividend payments. Dividend payments are a sign of legitimacy, and this is discussed further, later in the book. NORTEL pays a dividend for a certain class of shares but not the common stock that has been fluctuating wildly.

The Theory of Supply and Demand

The theory in the market works as follows, the more bidders for a stock the higher the price will be driven to meet the demand, as people who do not have their bid filled move to take out the offer, this move drives the bids and offers to higher levels. Of course, the theory works in practice that eventually a price point is reached where the demand is now cut off by the supply, too much supply, and no demand then means a falling price.

From my experience, I found rather than work the theory to the reversal point, allowing the price of a stock to move so high that demand ceases, and supply becomes huge due to everyone wanting to sell. The theory holds true that if demand occurs and supply is provided at the level of demand (the price point) or below that price point, shares at infinitum can be disposed of. Please note that it appears this is being played out by NORTEL as I write.

All scam deals will work the theory of supply and demand and will be successful for a period but eventually fail because the theory is a true state of affairs. The manipulator wants to dispose of shares he has at a good high price. It has been ingrained in the promoter's head to do that there has to be demand. The demand that occurs helps in the price being manipulated higher. Unfortunately, since the theory is correct in every way, there will always be a point unknown to anyone, where the price becomes a major factor in quelling demand. Around the same time, the supply available suddenly becomes more than the market can take.

This scenario is always played out in a manipulated deal, and in real legitimate deals the theory works the same way except the price reversal is not as great because real defined issues form the backbone of the real, legitimate deal.

Dividends, which are a yield on investment, form the backbone of a legitimate deals value. The reason the price reversal occurs is that for the price to truly rise to that point of reversal, there had to have been a manipulation upward. If there was no manipulation upward to this reversal point, the market of demand would continue, and a true supply would be available to feed the demand. In reality, not everyone wants to buy at the same time nor do they all want to sell at the same time.

This theory of demand and supply is always evident. As the manipulator in the scam structure deal will work on trying to move the price higher a demand must be created for the stock. The created demand is an unnatural demand, created by the manipulator bidding at each higher level once offered stock is sold. Concurrently, an unnatural supply is manipulated by offering stock at higher price levels, usually small uniform amounts of stock. This will result in the stock moving to a reversal point. It has always happened, and the reason is that the majority of deals follow the scam share structure coupled with the misinformed theory of having to move the stock price to a higher price to sell off. This price reversal will occur because too many offers and selling will occur at a price not foreseen by anyone. It can be 5 cents higher; it can be $1 higher. It is unpredictable because people are unpredictable.

To avoid the pitfall of the huge price reversal, I found that if the price was manipulated to a point of demand at a price level where that continual demand existed for a stock, no price reversal point is reached. Let us use NORTEL as an example again. The price point below $3.00 and especially in the range of $0.50–$3.00 has seen unbelievable demand, and it is being fed by supply. It continues to be fed because I believe someone has found out what I had over ten years ago, fill demand and continuously fill the demand and shares at infinitum can be sold, as long as the shares are sold below or at the demand price.

BREX type Canadian Scams

Brex was a monumental scam perpetrated using the typical scam deal structure. As the scam grew in popularity, the share capital grew and was eventually split. In the stock split for each share an investor owned, an additional share was given to that investor, free. The share price was cut proportionately to the share split and in the Brex case the stock continued to climb higher based on the promotion of the largest gold discovery the world has ever seen.

I presume the stock split coincided with the core group of manipulators owning a huge proportionate amount of the stock, giving themselves that more stock when the price reached a very high inflated value. With the split the price was that much more cut, for example a 5 for one split at $50/shares would give you that much more free paper and a trading price of $10/share. This lower price now would seem to be more attractive to Joe public thus inducing more buying. With demand sucked dry by trading at $50/share, demand increased that much more at $10/share.

Many blue chip stocks that pay dividends utilize this stock split form of creating demand. The stock split will be done when the demand for the stock pushes the price to a high level, usually a price reversal point. The stock split benefits those who purchased before the split as now additional shares are received, in the majority of cases the stock price will increase from the new lower price. Microsoft has in its short life span completed nine stock splits.

The stock will always rise higher, if investors were buying it for $50 they will buy more at $10. In the BREX case, I believe the insiders owned the majority of the stock when they split, and continued more financings to reload to sell into the demand. The failing in their deal was they started with too little share capital initially, so as the demand rose they could not fill the demand. The price rose higher and higher. To fill demand they had to reload with new stock by completing private placements and issuing stock options.

The tell tale signs of a scam were present. The factors to consider in this situation as well as many similar situations that occurred at the same time, and will continue in the future, were the following.

The first factor combines the typical scam deal initial share structure and the management track record that included bankruptcy declarations. Numerous of the manipulative factors that were described earlier in the book were also present. The most important factor to be wary of was the location of the project.

The project location in the Brex type scam was a foreign country, well outside of reach by any individual who could conduct due diligence. Even well out of reach for any consultant to probe the project on behalf of investors or mining companies. In most cases unbeknownst to a company exploring its own prospect, if a discovery is announced, there will always be someone who drops in on the property to take a look at the drill core, the visible rocks of the property. In most cases, it would be another company representative spying on this new find to ascertain the prospect type, etc.

In the Brex scam the prospect was located in a very isolated area of Indonesia. Similar types of scam deals during this time, but not gaining as much notoriety, had project locations in Africa and South America. The location is exotic, and so controls on work are hard to contain even by a legitimate mining company, even some local working on the prospect could be concocting results just to continue receiving a decent monthly stipend.

Another factor is, determine who is doing the work, or the detailed analysis. A reputable third party should do the work, or if by the company, the assaying and reporting should be conducted by reputable, certified third parties.

This particular Brex scam had the other more baffling factor of no dissent. It is common place for industry related individuals to prematurely pass judgment on 99% of all projects, mostly in negative terms, in this particular case no one had publicly commented on the outrageous claims being made by the company and it's staff. In most huge scams of days gone by this same factor is always missing.

Most notable factor has to be the greed factor. The amount of touting to the greed factor was huge. Claims of the largest gold deposit the world has ever seen, on a daily basis, and reserve estimates increasing by huge amounts every few days were illogical. The time factor of drilling and analysis and interpreting results was to close to prior claims that it would be impossible to increase reserves so fast.

The moment, well prior to the scam being found out, when the CEO declared he would rather lose the whole project rather than keep 50% as dictated to him by the Indonesian government was the moment I knew this deal was a scam. In all my years of dealing, and I know that any reasonable person would do the same, if a gun is held to your head and you are allowed to keep part of something or none of something, I would always take the part of something. This ploy by the CEO was in fact done to keep anyone with knowledge on gold prospects from visiting the site and reviewing the company's data, because he knew the scam would be found out.

As it later turned out, the buildings on site were burnt after the Brex had been forced to take a partner and after the new partner had found no gold in it's own test drill holes. Around the same time as the new partner found no gold in the drill holes, the chief geologist on the site was thrown from a military helicopter, I presume after disgorging the truth of the scam to high ranking Indonesians who were partners of the new partner.

Even when results of no gold were released to the public, every news outlet in Canada was in an uproar that the new partner, an American major mining company, was trying to steal the deal from the Canadian company. The newspapers continued to print and tell the management story of huge reserves, as the stock was clobbered from high $200/share down to pennies. I still cannot understand how the newspapers, editors, and reporters were never sued or taken to task by the authorities

From all my experience, when a lot of people that are involved directly in the industry bad mouth a particular deal, most likely the deal is real, when everyone is praising the deal, that is time to be wary. Of course when the major mining company came out and told everyone their drilling encountered no gold, that's not the time you apply this theory, that's the time the theory is proven right since everyone in the industry had touted the deal as legitimate.

Of course with that said, there have to be some red flags to look for that leave at least a bit of doubt in an individual investors mind. Public comments by the executives or working personnel that leave questions, or like in the Brex case do not make logical sense, should leave an investor leery of speculating in the deal. If you have huge amount of funds at your disposal that is the time to start short selling. However, expect a long haul before you see a return from the short selling.

Trading values reaching huge numbers, leaving a company with a huge market value when its underlying true cash and comparables value are much lower, are signs to avoid the deal to avoid financial disaster.

The factors present were the typical scam share structure, the exotic location of the project, the bizarre actions and comments, self promoting by executives, and the lack of reputable companies doing checks and analysis, coupled with managements total lack of prior accomplishments.

One major factor in looking at results and evaluating those results by the investor would be, in relation to the junior mining deal. Assay results should show a bit of variation in overall drilling of holes as well as each hole in particular. When nature disperses ores, it does not disperse them uniformly, the ores can be controlled by a structure, but the assay grades of economic metals cannot be uniform throughout, that is why averages are always taken, and always some areas within a deposit of any type of ore will be richer than others.

Confirmation of Results

As alluded to previously, there always will be some spying or third party skullduggery to ascertain the facts reported by a company to a new find. Other companies or even private investors will have an expert move onto a prospect sometimes in clandestine fashion to check the veracity of claims. In some cases new finds could be huge thus opening the way for large geological provinces to yield a number of deposits. If a new find suggests this type of potential then third party confirmations even without the original company making the find knowing will be attempted. In all instances, none of these issues will be publicly reported.

As another example I will tell you that when the Diamet diamond find had been announced and progressing the major mining company that was paying for the work, and taking the substantial interest was at first leery of the results. As a test, the Operations Manager obtained a large number and variety of rough industrial diamonds from a third party and salted a number of samples that the Diamet were evaluating. Diamet never reported the industrial diamonds that were used in the salting to the partner. This non reporting of the industrial diamonds provided a comfort level for the partner.

High Volume Trading, High-Priced High Capitalization scams

These particular types of deals generally trade huge volumes in very high-capitalized company's and trade for large dollar values.

The initial share structure of these types of deals are high share capital, usually in most cases a core few of individuals will own the majority of the shares. A business project will be acquired or developed with huge revenue and earnings potential. A financing is completed at a multi-dollar price level, giving the company a healthy share capitalization based on potential revenues. With the core group controlling the majority of the public float, high trading volumes are generated by large promotional campaigns.

The promotional campaigns could just be a large number of unwitting brokers calling clients to let them in on a new hot deal. As the volume and price movements suck people in, the price continues to be manipulated in an upward fashion, allowing the core group to dispose of their large holdings. False accounting numbers continually perpetrates the scam. These numbers generally tout large cash reserves on the balance sheet or high earnings totals. Even with high earnings totals net earnings are shown lower or almost none existent even within the financial statements. No dividends are paid and the scam deal due to the huge market following and huge trading volumes will continue to trade large numbers as individuals continue to buy and sell, but there is a long or even a sudden price slide. The executives will usually blame market conditions.

The factors in this type of scam to be leery of are the following. A large number of brokerage firms touting the shares to the public. Executives in the touted company with no real record of accomplishment of involvement in a large multi-national firm with relevant experience in the particular sector of the scam deal. Huge share positions controlled by a core group, received without payment of cash for the shares, or given to the core group at low prices compared to the IPO price.

The major factor to remember is this. In today's market place, it is common for an individual investment broker or banker having setup a fund with each individual client having 1 million dollars or more invested. If the investment banker has 100 of these clients, he has at his disposal 100 million dollars of play money. If you have 10 of these investment advisor characters come on board to play a deal, with perks-meaning gratuities given by the company, or worse even the investment banker having been unwittingly conned, there is over 1 billion dollars worth of buying power. Alternately, the market manipulation technique of attracting day trading will also attract these investment advisors who will unwittingly be playing a manipulated market helping in the disposal of more shares, again even just ten of these types of players in a high volume deal can help propel it much higher with much more volume.

This is not unheard of; the amount of volumes trading every day on any major stock exchange in the United States and Canada suggests that there has to be a huge number of investment bankers with funds of this size, and even mutual funds money at their disposal, to play with. With these huge bankrolls, it is logical to suspect that any high-capitalized stock can be manipulated to a higher level if a few of these individuals act in concert. Some are very smart and seeing a cohort trading in the stock, might cause them to jump on the bandwagon in that manner. In the end, the huge run ups of these high issued capital deals has to suggest a market manipulation when they collapse.

These deals again take into account the theory of supply and demand but again follow the scam model of the price manipulated to such a level so as the stock reaches a price reversal point.

Structure Of Financings Suggesting Scam Deals

In the typical scam share deal it was noted, usually the amount of capital issued is under 5 million shares. From the previous chapter I had mentioned the high volume high capitalization scam. To get the high capitalization scam moving, initially a large number of shares have to be in friendly hands. This is true if the price is to move to a high price. Consider that even at $1.00 or even $0.50 that 25 million or more shares would be a very high capitalized stock. The amount of shares that have to trade if there is a large shareholder base of free-trading shares would be huge to have the stock move higher. On the NYSE and NASDAQ it is not uncommon for a huge capitalization deal with a large number of shares owned by an insider group, with the stock price trading at much higher prices, $10.00, $50.00 or $100.00. The deal can be a scam, just substitute the higher price into the scenario as I have described previously.

The more shares in the hands of the manipulators the easier to move it to the higher price and the easier to sell off some of the large number of shares. As the position is offloaded and to avoid having to support the market the price is allowed to move lower, at each lower level more innocent people get sucked into the market of this stock. Eventually when the majority of shares are dispersed to a large shareholder base, and a high capitalization low price is present, the following would suggest a scam deal.

Additional shares can be created by the manipulator(s) in a combination of the following methods or all of these methods being employed. By issuing shares for debt, or for acquisition of the major product or research product, or just financings to insiders or insider brokers or offshore investors usually corporations owned through nominees by insiders or insider brokers via private placements or even by brokered secondary financings.

A prime example of a favorite method of financing the scam structured deal is by washing money and by completing shares for debt. Debt will be accumulated by insiders through, in most cases, inflated fees, usually involving administrative expenses, then shares are issued for eliminating debt. In Canada and on the larger USA markets shares for debt have to be approved by the regulatory agencies because the company can issue the stock. This fact does not stop this method of restocking a manipulators portfolio. For a share for debt to be approved, the debt has to be audited, not hard as expenses can be created an accounted for with bills and invoices.

In most instances, the shares for debt are blown off immediately after they are issued and approved for issuance by the regulatory body for any amount of money. If you learn one message from my book, please avoid any deal, emphasis on any deal, issuing shares for debt. This particular practice should actually be outlawed. The only reason someone will issue shares for debt is they have no other creative method of creating paper to sell. If they are not creative enough to create paper for themselves to sell, how in this world will they be creative enough to promote the stock to sell their own paper? How will you as an investor be able to ever sell your stock higher? In all instances, no promotion is even attempted just shares blown off into the market at any price. This is a loser deal; avoid this deal and any deal with the same individuals acting as promoter or directors.

The washing money scenario works like this. Money is received from a legitimate source for a financing, usually via a private placement, the funds are deposited into the company account, then are paid out to an insider or his nominee directly or indirectly thru shell companies or a legitimate company, for a product, or for eliminating a debt owed or for acquisition of an asset. The same money is then re-deposited back into the company account, deposited as part of a financing, thus increasing the financing from the original amount to an additional greater amount.

An example would be $50,000 contributed by Joe public to the company for a financing via private placement, but the $50,000 is washed out to the insider, then back in by the insider or nominee to the nominee or insiders content. If they wanted a $500,000 financing they would deposit the initial $50,000 in to the company account then wash in and out a further $450,000, using the $50,000, nine times in and out of the company account to then announce a $500,000 financing.

Using the same example above, the $50,000 can just as easily come from a manipulator or a nominee, with the same important fact of money in, credit, and money out, debit, being employed.

I suspect a recent notorious Vancouver figure J. "Jack" P., popularly known to promoters in Vancouver as "Gem Jack" would have completed this scenario a few times recently. I had a run in with Gem Jack in the late 80's; he was a gambler and a big scam man. He would bet on anything, I had a small plastic basketball hoop with a nerf ball in my office. One day J.P. and I threw enough baskets or, he missed enough, for me to have ownership of his Rolex Presidents watch, I felt sorry for him, can you believe it, and missed on purpose on double or nothing so I wouldn't take his Rolex plus $20,000.

J.P.'s notoriety hit an all time high in the summer of 2002 when the FBI arrested him during a sting operation called Bermuda Short. From reading the FBI's information, it appears J.P. thought he was dealing with a big drug dealer from the USA. The drug dealer wanted to launder his ill gotten gains and found J.P., among others, more than willing to do the washing. J.P.'s situation was a bit different in that he wouldn't take a fee like other scoundrels rounded up in the sting operation, instead he worked out an agreement with the drug dealer where for a few days Purdy could use the money to his whim and fancy as long as he wired back all the money. The FBI seems a bit astonished as to what could have happened, this is my take on the situation.

J.P. would launder money for the "drug dealer" and not take a fee but would instead be allowed to use the money for his own purposes for a number of days. I suspect the FBI can't figure out what he did with the money, I would suggest they look into how many financings, private placements, J.P. and his cronies and his nominee company's did in the time period of him receiving the money and laundering back to the "drug dealer". Without a doubt J.P. would have washed that money in and out of a few different listed company treasuries and loaded up big time on stock in deals getting setup to blow off paper.

This information on private placements would be available and would not take too much investigative time to determine. For an Auditor's sake the company announcing a private placement must show money deposited into it's account, then a Director of the Company will verify in a signed off document that monies for the private placement had been received. The Auditor for financial statements would see the deposit and know money was received and the added information from the Company (Directors letter) would confirm the money was received for stock to be issued.

The Company could deposit the money then re-issue checks to the individuals to cover debts or make loans to the individual for future debt. The money then could be used again for another Company private placement. With the funds totaling $500,000, private placements from $500,000–$1 million could be announced and completed for any number of Company's, all within one to two days, especially if the bank accounts for the Company's and Individuals receiving back the funds are within the same bank. After this series of transactions, the appropriate documentation for the Trust Company, Company Lawyers and Accountants would be drawn up and filed for the annual Audit.

With the insiders loaded up with new stock that cost virtually nothing they now have supply to feed demand, to convert the paper to cash.

As you can understand the principle of making money is not very difficult when you have created paper free.

With the huge interest in the stock market since 1996, I believe this is when the bull market started, with demand for any speculative deal incredible, it appears a large number of individuals would have took part in this financing scenario. Many of the high capitalization deals also seem to have followed the same type of financing scenarios. Numerous rollbacks and shares for debt would have been played out during this huge bull market run allowing many individuals to capitalize in a huge manner.

Offshore Havens

A popular procedure to avoid Enforcement detection of individuals pulling a manipulation off is for the individual to use nominees in off-shore havens, either individually or through the creation of a shell company to invest in the manipulated deal. Without doubt, you would have heard from news accounts in the past of an individual who has incorporated in the Cayman Islands, The Bahamas or the Turks and Caicos Islands, to name a few. Most likely, you have seen ads in newspapers especially in the classifieds section of a newspaper or a financial paper where a law firm is advertising incorporations in any of these or similar tax havens.

The manipulator/insider does this to avoid two scenarios. The first is to avoid having to declare on insider trading forms that the insider is selling thereby alerting the whole world to what is happening and secondly the thinking is that no taxes have to be paid on the funds realized. If the trading by the offshore nominee is being done, who can prove it is the insider? If a nominee conducts the trading, what individual can pinpoint the activity on the manipulator and thus how will he have to pay taxes on the money realized?

Both ways of thinking are wrong. The fact is the manipulator knows who the owner of the stock really is. If the manipulator were an insider, the manipulator would still be required to fill out the insider trading forms because he was selling the stock indirectly. In addition, if the manipulator is a resident of Canada or the United States he is still required by law to declare worldwide income, especially when the order to trade was initiated in either Canada or the USA.

The way a manipulator would work the situation of an offshore incorporation could involve a few scenarios. Most likely, the manipulator would find through the placing of such ads a Lawyer in the jurisdiction that he would like to incorporate a company or have a nominee. The nominee or the now incorporated company with any number of tax haven locals as director nominees would then take down financings or purchase shares privately from the manipulator at discounted prices.

Usually what transpires is the shell company would take stock by the cash in and cash out method and them sell off the stock into the market. The manipulator creates two handy situations, not having to pay tax on any profit and no one knowing who really is disposing of the shares. Of course the more sophisticated manipulators would create the shares through cash in and cash out method completing the financings at a price much higher than the current trading market and would dispose of the shares at a loss, saving himself a huge tax headache that would be created by the cash in and cash out share creation method.

A lot of times especially in a small town like Vancouver, individuals would have dealt with a lawyer in a tax haven, seen how easy it was to do the setup and take down a private financing, that they would undoubtedly pass along the name of the lawyer to a buddy who would be envious of his colleagues sudden success. If a raid were ever done on a few of these lawyers in the tax havens where a lot of private placements subscribed for by individuals or corporations residing in the particular tax haven jurisdiction were announced, the number of manipulators with nominees participating in the private financings would be eye opening to authorities and to the general public.

The Missing Factor Of A Scam Deal

The missing factor of a scam deal would have to be the one reason why it has been touted prior to the mid 1990's to invest in the stock market. The reason to invest is to earn a yield on your investment.

Throughout all the touting and the hot bull market run, on all the financial programs on television through the different medias, in the financial magazines and newspapers the old adage of investing for yield has been abandoned. Yield is the dividend paid by a company divided by its stock price.

It is not earnings or potential for earnings, it is not profit or potential profit it is not increased sales or potential increased sales, it is the dividend paid to you as an investor. These are the types of deals to invest in, blue chip scenarios, that are dividend paying firms. These deals give you an annual return on your investment that is in some cases very constant, with the added bonus to you, that perhaps the blue chip stock will appreciate in value, by interest rates falling thus the price of the dividend paying stock rising to have the yield match interest rates.

Any other investment is speculative in nature and leads to greed and to manipulation, as greed breed's greed. As an investor you are greedy trying to buy a stock moving up, the insiders are greedy as they see unheard of demand for their stock, so they become greedy on feeding the greed demand. That is what leads to these scam deals. Scam deals exist because of the vice of greed.

Since the stock market is a trading place, to make money you have to buy and sell stock, it is hard not to get greedy when demand for stock exists and prices move higher. If you are investing, you have to look for yield not speculative returns on stock price created by trading.

The missing factor in a scam deal is the dividend paid. This is true in all cases, and especially blue chips. Once as an investor you have been sucked into thinking earnings drive a stock price, that is when the public has been conditioned to buy speculative stocks, scam deals hidden as speculative deals.

During the editing of this book, President George Bush has put forward an economic package that includes tax cuts on dividends paid by companies. President Bush has put forward this proposal to counter, as I have been stating within the book, the nefarious activities of insiders and stockbrokers. President Bush stated that profits are opinions but dividends are fact. Soon after the economic package announcement, Microsoft announced its first dividend payment in history

The factors to determine a scam speculative deal have been dealt with early on, but the focus of an investor must be to realize a return on investment and the stock market principle has always been to buy stock which will give you a quarterly dividend, that cannot be matched by a bank. That is what a stock market is. The speculative deal is thrown into the mix to soak up your money with promises of huge returns. If it is not paying dividends it is speculative whether it is high cap or low cap or mid cap. If the factors aforementioned in earlier chapters are present then the speculative deal is a scam deal, no questions about it. The majority of the participants involved in the deal may not be the scammers but if directly involved in the venture they would have figured out the game plan.

The greed factor is huge during a bull market run. An individual hears of someone close to them making a windfall during the bull market run, gets inundated on a daily basis by the industry that is spawned by a bull market run, then the individual finally gets sucked into the bull market. While this greed factor grows in Joe public, the greed creeps into the company insiders.

As an insider, if you are involved in the market daily, it is not hard to see that the greed of Joe public has driven the market for your speculative deal. The common factor driving greed and speculation in the 1996 bull market run was earnings reports and potential for earnings. The more news speculating possible earnings, the more Joe public became involved in the market. With the majority of insiders turning a blind eye and participating in the issuance of speculative news releases, I would suggest the majority of insiders, of most blue chip speculative deals, that meet the majority of the disclosed market manipulation factors outlined earlier, would definitely be considered market manipulators.

Into that mix, I would throw the broker dealers, advisers, and investment analysts who continued to issue and churn out stories cultivating the greed in Joe public. These investment professionals helped to tout and hype stocks, manipulating them higher and at any and every opportunity continued to pump out information, the majority speculating as to earnings to be reported.

This greed mentality I would say was the driving force to price movement in the 1996 bull market. It did not take a brain surgeon to realize the driving force for Joe public speculating in stocks, jamming the prices higher with huge interest. All you had to be was an investment professional, more specifically a manipulator. If you wanted the deal you were involved in to attract the same type of Joe public attention then all you had to do was start spouting the same type of reports and speculative mumble jumble as a successful hype deal. The investment industry and corresponding support services since the early 1990's and more specifically since 1996 has grown exponentially. It is not uncommon these days to have two investment firms with office representatives in one neighborhood, every bank has investment specialists, and recently every insurance firm or mutual fund has it's own investment specialists pumping out information and advice and receiving their cut of the commission.

What has created this demand, this evolution of so many investment professionals deeming themselves to be professionals and experts? The answer is the 1996 bull market run and Joe public driving it based on speculative investing. Again, I will use my favorite saying, during a bull market, everyone can pick a stock and be successful, but when it comes to true investing principles will someone have the same amount of success? The answer of course is hardly. I would suggest being careful of even dealing with an investment professional.

Investment Professionals

The media outlets should also be blamed, to some degree as they continued and continue to be a platform for analysts and certain investment professionals stated market or stock recommendations, predictions. There should be more temperance in reporting this information, or a disclaimer. Sure, it is news that a certain analyst speculates a particular deal will appreciate in price, but there should a disclaimer or a different side put forward in each story. The main problem of course is the fact that the majority of reporters in these publications had never in the past participated in any successful venture or deal, or been involved in the real promotion of a deal. The majority of reporters are simply relaying to you what has been promoted to them by an investment professional. In most cases the reporting since 1996 centered on speculation surrounding earnings and speculative outcomes of a deal rather than based on fundamentals.

A major problem is the credibility factor, in a bull market, credibility falls to anyone who touted an earlier deal that of course became a huge high flier, never mind the fact it ultimately collapsed in price and revealed itself to be a sham of a deal. These individuals, most times, investment professionals, were suddenly deemed an expert.

These experts would continue to receive press and to substantiate their existence; the majority would focus on earnings potentials, as that is what seemed to be driving the market. Typically, it has always been deemed speculative investing to base your investing solely on the prospect of earnings. The experts that were being relied on were not providing sound investment advice. The majority of these reported on experts became conduits for the touting of deals that have eventually been revealed scam deals.

I would presume these experts themselves did not realize their touts were scam deals. They were of course caught up in the greed factor. Their advice was pumping deals higher and higher, and with the movement higher, the experts own worth would increase. They would continue the pace of recommendations using the same factors they had used on prior touts on the new tout. Most likely, they would have been shaking their head the first few times and could not believe how well the tout turned out. Then they would move on to the next tout, whether they had an interest in the deals or not is a moot point. I am sure that their ego swelled and thought himself or herself boy or girl wonder of investing, financial geniuses, or stock picking gurus. In essence, they were manipulators sucking Joe public hard earned money into pig deals.

I believe there is a huge amount of naivety that exists with the number of new investment professionals that moved into the securities market field since the mid 1990's and this contributed to the manipulators manipulating these individuals. The investment professional's argument would be the job description is to invest and make investment recommendations. For each trade the professional makes a commission and, if the professional invests in a deal directly and this deal skyrockets, they are entitled to the profits.

Being ignorant of true business valuations, on how to apply general formulas to value a potential investment, and what a true market is, the identifiers of a true trading market, should not be a defense utilized when defending against investors losing in scam deals. Nor should there be a defense that recommendations or advice was given because "it is my job to advise." In most instances when bad advise or recommendations become known, it is because the advisor has been duped and could not determine the scam. Many times they may be directly involved in the scam. It cannot be a defense, that "I was just doing my job," when someone gives advice on investments. Many times in recent time, the whole investment touted is wrong theoretically and is doomed for failure from the initial tout.

People were drawn to the profession to make money pure and simple. As an investor when your money is gone and everyone involved just shrugs their shoulders and says "oh well, that's the market, that's the investment market for you," I would suggest you do not take that answer. If any deal you invested in meets the scam factors outlined in this book I would suggest it was a scam deal, no doubt about it.

From my experience let me explain how investment professionals make their money.

As stated, the investment professional will receive a portion of the commission that is charged to complete a trade. In discount brokers, the investment professional will receive a standard wage, similar to an investment specialist with a bank or a mutual fund. In addition to the wage, most firms, banks, investment firms, insurance company's, mutual funds, will supply a bonus by way of a commission or by way of a reward.

In all instances if a reward or a bonus is given, this is never reported to you as an investor. In fact, if a stock promoter or manipulator gives a broker a reward, in most cases free shares in a stock, then if that is not disclosed the broker can be in big trouble, very big trouble. The same however is not true for insurance companies, mutual funds, investment companies, etc.

For instance, most investment company's, banks, insurance company's and mutual funds, will give an investment advisor, professional, a set commission fee for first bringing a clients money into the firm. Usually as high as 3%, plus for each year you keep your money at the firm, the investment professional receives a yearly fee of again as high as 3% of money on record under the professional's control. On top of this, if you invest in a particular product the professional receives an additional up to as high as 3% of the money invested.

Neither the firm nor the professional have to advise you of this.

The next method of a professional making money off you is to sell you a stock he owns. This is against all Securities rules. Unfortunately, it happens everyday. If the professional sells you a stock he must tell you, advise you he is selling you his own stock. If his nominee sells you the stock, there is no requirement to make the disclosure.

A favorite trick of the manipulator has been to grease a professional. To grease is to give the professional a fee or free stock to induce someone to buy the manipulators stock. In every instance of my experience watching this scenario unfold, never have I seen anyone benefit. I never participated in this practice, as most times on watching a loser promoter pull this tactic off, 10 times out of 10 the loser promoter ended up buying the stock back in the market, I suppose this would be a version of back dooring, in most cases though it simply is the fact the professional has no clients.

A favorite of professionals is the churning of an account. The majority of professionals if dealing in a speculative market will want to try to get the account of a promoter or manipulator. They are interested in the amount of trading activity and want to make the commission on all the trades. Additionally, they can even watch how the manipulator trades to maybe sneak in a few trades against the promoter or manipulator.

The churning of an account, involves having the client continually buy and sell stock so that the commission can be earned on each trade, eventually the account is churned so much that loss trades will occur simply to have a trade occur. Eventually the account is eaten up by the commission and the trading losses incurred, the money having found its way over to the professional through commission or even in some cases by selling the professionals stock to the unsuspecting client.

If you have ever dealt with a professional and seen how protective they are of their accounts, you would understand the mentality of the professional is "this clients money is my money, no one else is going to get their hands on it, it's mine." Even if you phone up and ask for a check the professional can become defensive, try to keep you from pulling your money, or try selling you on another deal.

If this happens, a professional trying to stop you in a subtle manner from taking your money or even a bit of it out of an account, you have a problem, and I would avoid dealing with this individual.

In Vancouver, the favorite past time of professionals was to try to build their client base, the book it is called. To accomplish this the professional needs new stock picks, high fliers that show good runs. In the financial business of speculative deals, one is only as good as the last deal. With a successful price movement the professional would contact his list of clients or potential clients to hype his winner, or make you recall, that at twenty cents lower or fifty cents lower he had mentioned this stock to you open an account for the next one baby. Of course, eventually the client would capitulate and entrust more money or new money to the account.

The best money marker would be participating in a new IPO, especially if the appropriate scam deal structure was implemented. In this case, the professional would earn the commission in selling the IPO, he would provide the minimum amount of shares to the clients, and when the deal skyrocketed, the professional could tout the client on his stock picking expertise. This method of touting would help pull more money into the next IPO he would complete which, of course, would have the same scam deal structure. In many cases where the professional would have been involved in the deal, indirectly, through a nominee, in most cases every effort would be done to curtail a client from selling stock when a client would want to. Of course, why would the professional want you to sell into the manipulated market or into his promoters market when the professional himself can fill the demand and pocket the money?

From following the big cap deals since 1996, it is obvious the Vancouver practices seem to have been utilized in every type of market including NASDAQ and NYSE. These practices are of course so simple in thinking and should be so easy to identify but there has always been reluctance on the part of enforcement to believe clients on this issue.

In reality, if a truly spectacular manipulation occurs, these tactics do not have to be involved, since the buying is attracted usually by volume and always by the manipulation of the market, and no strong arm twisting not to sell into the market have to be incorporated.

If you have a professional, I am not saying that is a bad situation; I am just explaining how the system works. To buy a stock or sell a stock you will need a professional, but the danger lies in listening to the advice or asking the advice of a professional.

In most cases, please remember, just because the professional is employed as a professional, and took some courses, or graduated with a degree, this degree does not make them a guru. They have to deal with all the market factors that I have put forward, and a professional can be deceived just as easily as Joe public. I would point out the reason I put this information together is to help you to conduct your own research, look under the fluff and avoid the scam deals.

Newsletter Writers

I include this information to make you aware of investment newsletter writers. This group of course again is as good as the last deal they touted in their newsletter.

The newsletter writers in almost all cases are paid by a promoter or manipulator to write the information about a company. The deals paying for the newsletter writer are of course paying for a story in his rag that is sent out to his list of subscribers or his mailing list. The more people seeing the stock recommended the more chances of one of the newsletter writers subscribers or their friends will buy the manipulators stock.

The newsletter writer also becomes more well known and the price to be included in his newsletter goes higher as the more stocks that end up getting manipulated way higher that he previously wrote about make him look more like a financial genius every day.

I kept this to its minimal level but this is exactly what happens. I know because I use to pay newsletter writers to include my company in their newsletter. Being included in a newsletter breeds more following from stock brokers that like to see a company promoted in this manner. Brokers will then start touting your deal to more people so that the professional can take some credit for telling an investor about the deal, when it was trading at lower levels.

What I have found most disturbing since 1996 was the fact so many brokerage house analysts were always receiving so much press to tout their stock picks. The analysts would be in a conflict of interest and yet no Enforcement action was taken against these people. The analyst would tout deals they or their firm had underwritten or had huge positions, creating some buying from the public that would have been sup-plied by their employer. How this is not seen as a conflict of interest is beyond me. This method is one of the favorite methods employed by a manipulator to help create a market in the stock. What investor is not going to follow a stock recommended by a huge investment firm ana-lyst, especially if all the bells and whistles were thrown into the report? As the manipulator moves the stock, the investors having read the report blame themselves for not buying and eventually are sucked into the market.

I found that many of the deals written up by stock analysts in Van-couver were actually deals the brokerage house owned stock in or had floated with stockbrokers involved in the deal. This practice continues today, it has not stopped. Even the Chairman of the local Securities Commission announced that he does not support the actions of the Securities and Exchange Commission in the USA in regards to placing rules on stock analysts. He recommends that Canada not follow the USA.

A lot of time my deals would be recommended without having to pay the analyst. This helped in promoting, only because we were active in exploring good prospects with joint venture partners who were major mining companies. The Analyst recommending in this manner is usually adding a few deals to their newsletters that appear to have a good chance of success. If the mentioned deals become successful, it builds credibility then it is easier to attract attention to another in house deal.

Enforcement Authorities

By the time you have read to this section, you know more than any Enforcement Authority knows today.

One point to remember is this. How can an enforcement official know what a scam deal is if the official has never participated in one or witnessed one. For that matter, if they truly knew what factors, as I outlined throughout this book, were present in a scam deal, without a doubt the officials would have stopped most of the scams from happening as they could stop them in progress. Where were all these officials when Enron, Nortel, or WorldCom were actively duping investors? Most were sitting in their office and playing on their computers wondering where all these huge amounts of regulatory fees were coming from.

In 1996, the local Securities Commission was receiving around 600 complaints a year, in 2001, there were over 6,000 complaints on average per year. The amount of complaints has grown as a percentage to the amount of participants in the markets.

The huge amount of participants in the markets who have been scammed in deals that run as the factors pointed out is phenomenal when at least 6,000 people will have filed a complaint. The question that has to be asked is how do the enforcement officials determine a legitimate complaint from a bogus one. Who decides which complaints are followed through on?

When you as an investor lose your money, there is no recourse where you can recoup your money immediately, or perhaps ever. It would take you a fortune to sue in Court and it will take a lot of loud noise to have Enforcement Officials to progress on a case. All you will get from everyone is first the questioning of your credibility then a shrug of shoulders and an "oh well." In most cases, take the approximate figure of 6,000 people locally who file complaints annually. Enforcement would proceed to investigate approximately 10 cases. The question is always asked how do Enforcement decide on what cases to investigate and proceed on, and which to ignore.

From my experience the chances of a complaint proceeding to investigation is very remote. Enforcement will only investigate complaints against someone they have previously investigated and were unable to find any wrongdoing. It is the old "we know the individual is a nefarious type so lets get him." Alternatively, if a complainant has a contact with someone within the Enforcement Agency then a complaint will proceed. Any other time Enforcement will give you a shrug, a verbal sympathy and most times in reality will view you as a deserving victim as you are to blame as much as the one who defrauded you.

As an investor, receiving the shrugged shoulder, and the oh well, or the verbal sympathy doesn't really help you when the hard earned money put into what you thought was a legitimate deal a good investment or a good speculation is lost forever is not very welcoming. The reason the crooks are called con men is that they gain your trust. I have shown you the facts to look for that will alert you to a scam.

It is determining the existence of the factors I have outlined in this book that will save you your money. Of course an outright bad investment, timing of investment and market conditions can also effect your investment dollars, but if you research properly looking for the factors I have outlined then you can feel fairly certain and safe that your investment dollars are not being put into a sham deal.

A most important fact to remember is this. No Enforcement official has ever conducted or been a part of a scam deal or a sham deal. None have ever worked in the industry in the areas that would allow them to find out how a company is structured the way it is, nor can they imagine how to create paper without paying for it, nor can they conceive how to trade stock to have people show up out of the blue to buy the paper. In almost all cases, the charges are for obvious and apparent unsophisticated situations. They cannot understand a sophisticated scenario and in most cases never find real culprits.

Two good final facts to end this chapter are these.

A Securities Commission can employ newspaper columnists. I witnessed a well known local newspaper columnist, David Baines entering the local Securities Commission offices. What was so shocking was the fact he walked off the elevator, walked over to the secured access door and nonchalantly entered in an access code, he entered without a brief case or jacket. Mr. Baines writes on Securities scams, issues, and personalities. It is obvious from this encounter where he gets his information.

The second fact is this. During my Tribunal hearing in 1994, during the lunch breaks I would take the two hour break by visiting little Italy in Vancouver and watch the World Cup soccer games that coincided with my hearing. I would indulge in a good pasta lunch, then return to the inquisition. On each lunch hour break, I would saunter back and notice all three of the Tribunal members dining in the authentic Chinese restaurant downstairs from the Tribunal setting. What was so shocking and disturbing was the fact the Securities Commission lawyers, Director and Investigators would all be eating and cajoling together at the same table. This certainly was not a good sign where one expects a fair trial and justice to prevail. Another disturbing point was the fact that one member of the Tribunal was a South African expatriate Lawyer who had been with a large Law Firm in that country. Without doubt, he could not understand human rights issues.

Financial Statements, reading Stock Charts

The following factors to look for in Financial Statements refer to both speculative investments and high cap deals, as the same factors would be present in similar types of deals that are scam or sham deals. Now a high cap deal with years of continued operations could suddenly fall victim to some sort of fraud that eventually affects the stock price so be wary. The factors I outline will save you grief, anxiety, and sleepless nights.

Now of course if Financial Statements are fabricated you could lose sight of some important points. Most importantly, I will again tout the Dividend angle as you will recall investing in a stock market listed company has always been to keep your investment as safe as can be and realize a yield on the money you have invested. Dividends paid offer a yield, and these can be viewed on the daily trading charts in all financial newspapers, the true financial newspapers, like the Wall Street Journal, The Investors Business Daily, and in Canada The Financial Post. The basic trading chart of the Wall Street Journal follows the pattern as described.

Reading Stock Charts

On the first page of the Charts at the very top will be the name of the Stock Exchange for which the trading charts have been supplied. All companies listed on this Stock Exchange will be listed in the charts, on occasion a particular stock could be missing due to technical errors, but otherwise every stock listed will have traded on the Stock Exchange named for that particular day. The top row will have 52 week high, 52 week low, Stock, Ticker, Div, Yield percentage, P/E Vol, High, Low, Close, Net change. The 52 week high and low are self explanatory. The Stock refers to the name of the stock. Ticker refers to the ticker symbol. Most importantly, next comes the Div referring to the last dividend paid. The Yield percentage refers to the yield this particular stock on this particular trading day would return if you had bought it at the Close price. I have focused on the Dividend and Yield percentage as your investing guide. The Yield percentage as described in the daily chart will be the last dividend paid divided by the Close price for the stock on that day. If you bought this particular stock on the day of the chart at the Close price, all economic factors being equal, you should expect a yield on your investment of x percent on a yearly basis.

Of course as mentioned, if all economic factors remain the same, you could experience either an increase or a decrease on the yield dependent on numerous external economic pressures, but of all investments, investing for yield is the only investment to make.

Banks will give you a yearly interest rate, a Bank investment yield, on your deposits, and these rates are always quite discounted to what the Central Bank of a Nation will have set as a national bank rate. The national bank will be charging the banks for the yearly interest of providing national currency to continue daily operations. Your money once deposited of course is not sitting in a bank vault but is noted on a ledger a statement somewhere. For banks to issue cash against transactions on a daily basis the national bank of the country will ship out currency from a reserve to all the banks in the region so as enough money is on hand. This money is charged at a rate that is set by the Central bank, in the US it is the Federal Reserve in Canada it is the Bank of Canada. This rate can fluctuate on a weekly basis as occurred in the early 80's or on a quarterly basis as seen in present day.

Why I have gone into this fact is the point that the Central bank controls interest rates and that is where all institutions set their investment bank rates, and all financial instruments by. If you were receiving a 1.5 percent rate for your savings at a bank now you would be very lucky. For each $100 you will receive $1.50 in interest one year later. Whereas on October 25, 2002 if you had purchased 100 dollars worth of Disney stock your dividend yield would be 1.2 percent. However, if on the same day you purchased General Motors stock for each $100 you would receive a 5.2 percent yield.

Again, Disney and General Motors are two companies in different sectors with different economic factors pushing the amount of money they will make on a yearly basis, but these yields are in line or way above what you would receive in a bank.

As interest rates are raised by a central bank, the prices of companies like Disney and General Motors should fall to keep the dividend rate in line with the central bank rates. Likewise, if the rates a re lowered the prices for a stock will go higher to narrow the yield percentage the bank will pay you for your savings and what the dividend yield of a blue chip company like Disney and General Motors will pay out.

One more sound investment would be Bonds, Government bonds that trade on secondary markets. These are also reported on a daily basis and range in price levels and also in expiry time lengths, as well the yield on the bonds will be a few percentage points of each other, again based on length to maturity of the bond. The reason you are buying stock is for a safe return on your investment, a dividend. Dividends cannot be fabricated, either they are paid out as a dividend, or they are not. As I had quoted President Bush earlier, "profits are opinions, dividends are facts."

Reading Financial Statements

Financial Statements are a synopsis of a company's financial affairs for a particular time. All jurisdictions require that Annual Audited Financial Statements be supplied for continued listing. In Canada and on some exchanges in the USA Quarterly Financial Statements are required but these are not audited. Audited refers to the financials being Audited by a Certified Accountant as to the generally accepted accounting principles.

Generally accepted accounting principles are defined and may not be what an individual investor assumes this to mean. The generally accepted accounting principles are defined and are homogenous but that does not mean there cannot be dastardly goings on.

When an Audit is done, it usually means the company provides the yearly financial paperwork for the auditor along with in house completed financials. The larger the corporation and the more dealings the more likely the Auditor is to just pick and chose certain dealings to confirm the accuracy. If there is a problem then a more detailed Audit will take place, otherwise the statements are issued. In all cases, not every little transaction that could be material is declared as a note to the financials so some of the tricks to watch for are as follows.

On the Balance sheet a lot of times, there will be a position for loans or overpayment or advances or payables due, these notations in most cases relate to monies owing to an individual involved in the company and the money has been paid out as a loan or an advance or is owed.

Payables due indicate money is owed most likely to an individual involved with the company and if the debt continues to be included on several statements over time, it is being accumulated to eventually complete shares for debt. It can also most likely mean that real money is owed to real people for services rendered. Eventually if the debt is growing or still on a few statements over time most likely there will be a shares for debt regardless of who is owed money or a money wash in and out will be done concurrently with an announced private placement to reduce the debt and to reload with stock.

These notations usually always indicate a problem with the company, a deceptive situation occurring, immediately avoid these situations.

On the Statement of Profit and Loss, the yearly expenses are outlined. The expenses can be broken down or can be lumped into a few generic categories. Most important is to compare the administrative expenses on a yearly basis, wild fluctuations point to problems. Look for huge fluctuations in a certain category, usually look for management fees and for fees for an industry related to an industry of a individual listed as a consultant to the company or a director or officer of the company, or an accountant or lawyer of the firm. The fees would be directly going into this persons pocket, and reflect a bad situation, again avoid these situations immediately.

Review the section on expenses related to the workings of the company. The direct expenses related to the company's business at hand. If there is a fluctuation on a yearly basis or there seems to have been a huge amount of activity without any reporting of a spurt in exploration or research or manufacturing or an allowance over the time period through news releases for disclosure, then you have a problem and avoid this deal. An example of this would be the fact an exploration company has suddenly grown the expenses in both the administrative expenses and the working expenses but throughout the period covered in the financials never reported on work being conducted or reported on work that could never have covered the expenses audited.

Some very real examples are these.

A well known local Vancouver Lawyer was directly involved with a company purported to be building vehicles for sale in a Communist Country. The lawyer was billing for legal fees, was a director of the deal with all disclosed in filing documents. Look at the factors immediately outlined. This case had the factors of a professional billing directly for legal fees, being a direct insider and the deal having the prime business facility in an exotic locale. I forgot to mention the fact he was a director of a few other deals at the same time.

Glaring errors within the Audited Financial Statements suggesting scam, was the fact that prices for vehicles were given however the number of each vehicle sold did not add up to the number it should have been. For example a dr54x, sells for $5,000 and 543 of the vehicles were sold for a number that would equate to $2.715 million dollars. However, the number provided was much different than the simple multiplication. As well, inventory was included in the financials but did not match what was noted earlier in the prospectus document as having been produced. No accompanying notes to clarify the situation existed. Simple multiplication errors do not occur. All the errors suggested this was a manipulated document.

I bring this situation to your attention as I was given the information to look over and immediately on review of the information shook my head in disbelief. I myself approached the Local Commercial Crimes unit of the RCMP, brought the information to the attention of a staff sergeant, and pointed out the glaring discrepancies. The staff sergeant told me he knew the lawyer and he was a good person. I said well the facts do not lie.

The Exchange the company was listing on, actually sent over the president of the exchange and a director of enforcement to look at the operation. There is a picture of the two with some others standing in the purported factory smiling broadly. This particular picture was used in the exchange brochure, as the company was the first to be listed on this local exchange and to be traded in US currency. Without a doubt, the Lawyer involved in the company would have been promoting this fact and brochure when the company was trying to market the stock to US citizens. What better avenue to promote to US citizens, a car factory in China selling automobiles to Communist citizens, and to make it easier to understand the price, the stock trades in US currency.

Well once I saw the brochure and the short timing of the trip after my complaint I am certain the staff sergeant had passed along my concerns and the lawyer being with the in crowd at the exchange devised the scheme of sending over officers to legitimize the operation.

The fact the two went over and were hoodwinked is still beyond my comprehension. In due diligence, even major corporations when placing a huge order with a company will visit and conduct an onsite audit to ensure no shenanigans as this is the oldest trick in the book, visit our factory. The picture told a thousand words in this particular situation as no workers were seen in the background and no car was shown. Unbelievable, especially when the Audited Financial Statements listed inventory and the prospectus disclosed an ongoing operation.

The company listed and traded sporadically however a large amount of IPO cash was raised. The company eventually was delisted with investors never seeing a price rise, or the return of their money.

I reported the company to the Federal Bureau of Investigations and to the Securities Exchange Commission in the United States at the time. This glaring situation was never fully investigated, however as an investor if you had the benefit of the factors I have outlined in this book you would have immediately avoided this situation. The Securities and Exchange Commission however did acknowledge in a written letter that the matter was put on file. The FBI contacted me also and requested I visit the local representative of the FBI who would accompany me to visit the RCMP. I did not see how this would help so I did not follow through with the contact as I had already contacted the RCMP commercial crimes unit.

Audited Financial Statements will have the same information in similar form in different areas of the statement, watch for the similar reporting and make sure the numbers are the same, if the numbers are off it could be a mistake but if the statements are Audited these errors should be caught so avoid these deals. Avoid them because it would show a lack of care on the Auditors side if the least, and this is just as bad as false reporting as you cannot trust the statements.

Market Disclosure

To point out another scenario where having friends in the right places helps one avoid any type of scrutiny or penalty.

It has recently been reported that well over five years ago during a significant diamond find in the Nunavut Territory that has now commenced producing diamonds a two carat rough diamond was found protruding from drill core. The individual who was in charge of the exploration project also owned a large share position in the particular junior exploration company. On reviewing drill core, this individual now has disclosed five years after the fact, that the two carat diamond was intersected and visible in the drill core. What makes this fact so much more fascinating is that contrary to the disclosure rules at the time regarding material facts, there never was any public news release announcement of this fact made public. Only insiders and their friends would have known about this fact and actually, no one would have known of this fact if it were not recently reported.

The Market is about Emotions

If you are speculating then, watch for the factors outlined, and be wary if you decide to try to play the deal because you know it is a scam deal and you want to ride the market.

The market is all about emotions. Investing is emotional. It should not be emotional, but it is your money so it is impossible to not be emotional about investing. Since you know the factors present of a scam deal, what will stop you from suddenly hammering bids out? From all this information, you know the deal is a scam so you will be watching the market like a hawk. Anything could set you off to start the blow off and price retreat. Small bid sizes do not allow for an early escape by selling. Your emotions will play with you too much knowing what you now know and watching the market. What if you get panicky how do you know what will happen when you decide to sell out your position, will the stock get hammered down to the point of no return? How will you know when the manipulator(s) decide it is their level to be selling? How do you know whether one of the manipulator(s) is back dooring the deal?

Well you do not know the answer to any of those questions so the best case scenario is to avoid a scam deal when the scam factors are present.

Comprehensive Review Service

If you would like a review of a particular stock you can visit my website and put in a request. I will thoroughly review a deal and supply a detailed report. There is a fee for this service posted on my website. The website address is **www.marinospecogna.com**. There are stock charts with known manipulated stock deals also shown, so you can compare the technical charts of these scam deals with the deal you are interested in.

IPO Financings

With the huge bull market, IPO financings skyrocketed in popularity. More new issues were created to take advantage of the huge amounts of investment dollars in the public hands.

The large number of IPO's since 1996 focused on the high tech sector and other sectors that had huge earning potential, since earning potential was the speculative segment of the market.

The IPO deals would have followed the share structure for a few insiders receiving a large number of shares for introducing the technology, product, or idea to the company. The share creation using the cash in cash out method would occur at the initial stages of the company. In many of the cases, the broker dealer would take shares in the private stage, and then an IPO would be completed. The broker dealer would distribute the minimum number of shares to the public and would have all the brokers in the brokerage house tout the deal. The deal would be compared to other previous high fliers and would have the earning potential touted.

The demand in the after market would be a good strong demand, with a lot of the initial private stock held in escrow agreements the real market would be a few tradable private financing shares and the IPO shares. The majority of the IPO shares would be distributed to the broker dealer and insiders and these would be sold into the demand created for the stock. Of course, the price would be manipulated to a higher level to blow the shares off, because if only a portion of the stock owned that could be traded, with the majority of shares held in escrow agreements, then a higher price for the shares would be sought.

Manipulated deal pitfalls

Once you have read the information in this book to this point you will have enough expertise to pinpoint manipulated deals and if you use your head you will avoid these deals. Some of you though will be inclined to use this knowledge to play a manipulated deal knowing it is manipulated.

Without doubt, you can spot a stock manipulation now; the problem lies in attempting to play a manipulated deal. Usually only the manipulator or the group involved in the manipulation will know exactly what the game plan for the manipulation will be.

Recall that manipulators create stock free and dispose of the stock for financial gain. The more sophisticated manipulators can rock a stock up and down a few cents, lure an investor in, and continually dispose of stock. The price may look like it can continue higher but since the manipulator continues to dispose of shares that were created with no money the price the manipulator can sell at is any price.

The deals that are low cap and trading at low prices with previous roll backs or very limited trading volume do not have a sophisticated manipulator so there would never be any hope of seeing a stock run up.

When you determine a manipulation the best advise I will give you is avoid the situation. The only option would be to short the deal, but in most deals with the market psychology this could be a problem if you have limited funds available for the shorting. The problem I have seen is when a manipulator has created so much enthusiasm and sold off so much stock they simply run out of available shares to sell, if this occurs before the manipulator can reload with stock the price could burp up, and that is when you would be bought in.

The best use of this information would be to detect a manipulated deal and just avoid them. If you are unsure of a deal, visit my website at **www.marinospecogna.com**, and review the available services with associated fees.

About the Author

I grew up in small communities, places where at times the population ranged from a few thousand down to 50 inhabitants. My family later moved to a community with a population of 50,000 when I was around nine years of age.

The remote Queen Charlotte Islands, my birthplace and home to my first nine years of existence, are better known for the native Indian population, the Haida, of which I would say less that 500 inhabit the Islands. Wood production is and was the major industry with commercial fishing second, and maybe today, natives selling their carvings in large quantities to tourists or dealers.

My father was an Italian immigrant coming to Canada in the late 1940's. Numerous relatives had been living in Canada since the early 1900's. He emigrated from Italy, where he participated in the Second World War backed by the OSS, the CIA precursor, via the coalmines of Belgium. In Canada, he worked as a coal miner until the local coalmines closed down then he worked as a logging contractor. He still brags he had the west coast logging record, sometime in the early 1960's, falling over 13 million cubic feet of lumber in a twelve month period, mostly 1,200 to 1,800 year old trees on the Queen Charlotte Islands. Enough lumber to build one thousand 2,000 square foot homes. I have pictures of my two sisters, my mother, and myself with room for another four or five people on the cut stump of a one thousand five hundred year old tree my father had logged sometime in the early 1970's.

Wood production was so ingrained in every ones daily lives, in the early 1970's, that my buddies and I at this young age would try to emulate our fathers by logging on the weekends or after school. Without any parent knowing we would take an axe or two and go into the woods near our houses and start cutting small sized trees. This all ended one spring day when we were around eight, because my neighbor buddy, and one of his younger brothers, there were over eight kids in his family, went out logging by themselves. Good ole Jake tripped just as his younger brother was letting the axe come down. Jake got the axe stuck in his skull. We saw his mother run in to the only corner store to get more towels while Jake sat in the passenger side seat of the car. We had enough time to run over to poor Jake and ask how he was feeling. His head was wrapped good, and he said he was ok. The ride to the hospital was over 50 miles away, and in those days in the remote areas, all men were working and there were no emergency services. Jake survived and gave us all a good story to talk about. He at the time was already anti social so I do not think the axe affected him in any way.

On weekends, my father would prospect for gold. He became really good at it, so good that in 1979 his first major gold discovery became a worldwide headline. Hell even People magazine converged on our home and interviewed us all. We were the first citizens of Nanaimo, BC on Vancouver Island to be featured in People, probably even in the whole of British Columbia up to that time. Since then there have been a few other Nanaimoites given press in People Magazine, the famous jazz pianist Diana Krall, who attended the same high school and senior high school as I did is one person of note.

Those days in 1979, of reporters and television show reporters swarming our place was quite a show, there were even reporters from Europe. Numerous TV programs did small stories on my father, and we were able to take part in the small productions. The bigger story was the stock in the company, a small nothing deal before this project, skyrocketed from 7 cents a share to a high at one point of $22.00 per share. This had all coincided with the rise of gold from US$35 an ounce to over $700 an ounce.

The gold discovery in the Queen Charlotte Islands was found to contain over 3.0 million ounces of gold. The discovery was made in the early 1970's, and several major mining companies drilled the project during the early 1970s. Within two years of the discovery being made in 1970, a nice mineable reserve had been delineated, this would have been around 1973, of course with such a major prize, every one wanted to steal the deal. It would be found later, that the deposit was 10 times larger and richer than the major mining companies had put forward in reports back in 1973/1974. Years later, everyone involved claims someone mistakenly added a zero immediately after the decimal points for assay grades. Someone, no one seems to know who.

Due to politics, specifically native land claims issues; the deposit still has not begun to be mined. As a kid, around eight years old, my two sisters, my mother, my father and my uncle, mined a few tons of high-grade gold material. For us kids it was a fun weekend in the remote wilderness picking up white pieces of rock (quartz) and dropping it into big diesel barrels, or shoveling crushed material into one end of a sluice box, and seeing all the tiny little gold flakes appear on the bottom of the box. Gold fever is real and affects everyone, much the same as stock market fever.

I was very active in athletics, throughout high school and senior high school I was an integral member of several championships winning soccer, and basketball teams, as well as winning in individualized athletics. Team sports and athletics helped me learn to think while undertaking a task, it helped me learn what it takes to win and how hard it is to win something, to persevere to see something to fruition and how to work as a team to be successful. I was also voted president of my schools on a number of occasions, as well as winning academic and citizenship awards.

Having been involved in the mineral exploration field I decided to pursue this area of studies and graduated with a diploma in Mining Engineering Technology. I ended up in the stock market by raising funds for exploration of our projects and to promote our deals. In almost all cases, other parties always tried to take advantage of my age and supposed naivety to try to swindle me. Having been involved in sports, and knowing what a true team player is and what it takes to win, I always simply turned the tables on scoundrels.

From 1986 to 1996, I successfully completed a number of joint venture agreements on prospects owned by my companies with major mining companies, Inco Ltd., Noranda Ltd., and Teck Ltd. A number of new prospects were found. In total, since 1986, well over $50 million in exploration expenditures occurred on our projects or joint venture projects. Funds spent by crews working the prospects would have flowed into the small local economies that were near to the exploration sites.

In 1996, a decision was returned against me. Guilty. Convicted and according to the local Securities Commission I am worthy of the sentence delivered. In reality before a true court, a plea agreement was entered where I pled guilty to failure to file insider trading reports. What I have documented are shenanigans, inside secrets, that stock manipulators use to manipulate stocks, to scam people of their hard earned money. These shenanigans I learned by being in the midst of the desperados and bandits for over 10 years. The difference between a desperado and a bandit is distinct. The bandit is a thief but already having money, and the desperado has no money but is willing to do anything to get it.

I have found a lot of times the good and the bad guys can be easily mistaken by the amount of credibility an individual has and the amount of prejudices an individual has in making a determination of a good and a bad guy.

I would recommend reading both The Art of War by SunTzu, and The Prince by Machiavelli, both these books written ages ago, really do reflect human nature. Reading both will prepare anyone fully for business and even life dealings. In a final note, as Machiavelli states, when dealing with power reason will not prevail.

Terms Used

Account churning involves an investment professional continually buying or selling a clients account even taking losses to create commissions for the investment professional.

Ask is the price an individual is willing to sell a share.

Aftermarket refers to the trading market once a company has completed an Initial Public Offering.

Back dooring refers to the fact that a manipulation can consist of a group of individuals, when one of these individuals' sells against the manipulation this is considered back dooring.

Bid is the price at which an individual wants to purchase a share.

Blue chip stock deal, refers to the upper echelon of trading stocks in the world that are distinguished from other stocks in the fact that these blue chip stocks pay stock dividends, they are the premier stocks in the world.

Egregious meaning conspicuously and outrageously bad or reprehensible

Escrow agreement refers to a regulatory imposed agreement on individual shareholders of a public company to keep a large portion of their share holdings under control from selling. Usually a fraction of the total shares are released from the escrow agreement at dates set by the agreement.

Investment Professional refers to any individual licensed to buy or sell securities in a Regulated jurisdiction.

IPO refers to Initial Public Offering. This is the distribution of shares to the public by prospectus. The prospectus is approved by a regulatory agency and the stock exchange that is listing the company stock for trading. A broker dealer is the sponsor of the IPO and receives a disclosed commission for distributing the shares to the public. Once the IPO is completed, the shares commence trading on the exchange.

Jitney trade is a trade conducted by an individual with a brokerage account at one firm directing the trade through another firm, usually this practice is done to hide which house is selling the stock, to spread selling through several different brokerages to keep investors guessing as to who maybe selling. An extra cost is associated with this in commission fees, and it is not unheard of to complete a double jitney trade. In some cases a lot of the traders will know each other at smaller firms so directing a trade through a couple of large national houses will stop people from comparing notes.

Joe public refers to an individual from the public drawn into buying a stock.

Liquidity refers to the amount of stock trading on a daily basis. Good liquidity would mean in relation to all other stocks trading in the stock market the stock has top 25 trading status in terms of volume of stock traded on a daily basis.

Lot size is the size of the bid or offer, the amount of shares on the bid or on the offer.

Market means the price level at which a stock trades; the level where a third party individual will buy a share of a company, the trading price between a bid and an offer.

Phone monkey refers to any person working out of a boiler room and working on the phone, younger phone monkey's are referred to as phone chimps also alludes to the fact they still are quite naïve in what they are selling.

Promoter refers to an individual not licensed by any Regulatory Agency, in all Prospectus disclosures this term would refer to all Directors and Officers of the Public Company, who is in the business of putting forward a favorable view of the company to the general public and Investment community.

Prospectus refers to a detailed legal document, approved by Regulatory Agencies in a specific jurisdiction, disclosing all material information and Audited Financial Statements of a public company seeking to raise additional funds. In the United States a Prospectus is only required if raising funds over a certain threshold as mandated by the United States Securities Exchange. Within Canada, the stock exchange listing the shares as well the Provincial Securities Commission having jurisdiction would have to approve this document. This document is used by a public company when it is conducting an IPO to coincide with an application to have shares listed for trading on a Stock Exchange.

Reporting Issuer is any public company that is required to file documents with a Regulatory Agency.

The Crown refers to the Federal Government of Canada prosecuting individuals in the name of the Queen of England who is also the Queen of Canada. In all criminal cases, or any case involving either the Provincial Government or Federal Government and any of the legislation passed by those governments the government appointed solicitor is referred to as representing and acting for The Crown.

Tout is a term used in stock promotion meaning to praise, to sell, and to talk highly of in glowing terms.

0-595-26466-2

Printed in the United States
1144400004B/299